Building A Children's Chapel

One Story at a Time

BILL GORDH

CHURCH PUBLISHING
an imprint of
Church Publishing Incorporated, New York

A record of this book is available from the Library of Congress.

Church Publishing Incorporated
445 Fifth Avenue
New York, NY 10016

www.churchpublishing.org

5 4 3 2 1

TABLE OF CONTENTS

vii Acknowledgments

viii Foreword

x Author's Preface

PART ONE Creating the Framework for Chapel

3	Chapter 1	Setting Up Chapel	

PART TWO Stories of Self

			Songs
21	Chapter 2	Creation The Joy of Creativity	You've Got Me (s-a) * It Was Good
27	Chapter 3	The Garden of Eden Consequences and Learning from Mistakes	In My Garden (s-a) Would You Like to Take a Bite? (Snake, Adam, Eve)
35	Chapter 4	Noah and the Ark Faith and Working Together	*Arkie, Arkie* ** (s-a)
41	Chapter 5	Jonah and the Whale Doing What You Know You Should Do	*Who Did Swallow Jonah?* (s-a) I Don't Wanna Go to Nineveh
47	Chapter 6	Jesus and the Three Fishermen Persistence and Trying New Ideas	Keep On Trying (s-a) Peter and John and James

* (s-a) sing-along song
** Song titles in italics may be found in numerous other sources

53	Chapter 7	Jesus Heals the Sick Saying Thanks	I Want to Thank You (s-a)
57	Chapter 8	The Good Samaritan Helping Others	You've Got Me (s-a) Lend Me a Hand
PART THREE		**Stories of Family and Friends**	**Songs**
65	Chapter 9	The Naming of the Animals Friendship	You've Got Me (s-a)
69	Chapter 10	Abraham and Lot Sharing	Work a Little Bit (s-a)
75	Chapter 11	Joseph and His Family The Importance of Family and Forgiveness	Love Begins with Giving (s-a) Go Away! Once a Brother, Always a Brother
83	Chapter 12	Ruth and Naomi Friendship	You've Got Me (s-a) Wherever You Go
89	Chapter 13	Joshua and the City of Jericho Faith and Working Together	*Joshua Fit the Battle of Jericho* (s-a)
95	Chapter 14	Jesus Calls His Disciples Working Together	Work a Little Bit (s-a) Great Big Job
103	Chapter 15	The Lame Man Walks Helping Each Other	You've Got Me (s-a)
PART FOUR		**Stories of Faith, New Life, and Celebration**	**Songs**
109	Chapter 16	David and Goliath Faith in God and the Power of Poetry and Song	You Can Sing about Anything (s-a) *Little David Play on Your Harp*
115	Chapter 17	Moses and the Pharaoh Faith	*Go Down, Moses* (s-a)
121	Chapter 18	Daniel in the Lion's Den Faith	*Daniel in the Lion's Den* (s-a) I Want to Thank You (refrain)

129	Chapter 19	The Christmas Story	*Silent Night* (s-a)
		Celebration of Room for Us All in the Love of God	No Room at All
135	Chapter 20	Blessings for Baby Jesus	Love Begins with Giving (s-a)
		Celebration and Hope for Our Children	Blest Be the Child (Anna, Simeon, children)
141	Chapter 21	The Last Supper and the First Easter	Love Begins with Giving (s-a)
		Faith and Carrying On	

PART FIVE Stories of the Value of All Living Things — **Songs**

147	Chapter 22	The Parable of the Lost Sheep	Everything Counts (s-a)
		Value of Each Individual	Sleep, Sheep, Sleep
153	Chapter 23	Jesus and All the Children	Everything Counts (s-a)
		Importance of Children	Come unto Me
159	Chapter 24	The Parable of the Sowers	In My Garden (s-a)
		Taking Care	Sow Your Seeds
167	Chapter 25	The Parable of the Mustard Seed	Everything Counts (s-a)
		Importance of All, Regardless of Size	Take a Look

PART SIX Stories of Giving and Forgiving — **Songs**

177	Chapter 26	Two Little Fish and Five Loaves of Bread	Love Begins with Giving (s-a)
		Generosity	
181	Chapter 27	The Three Kings and the Young Girl	Love Begins with Giving (s-a)
		Giving	My Gift Is Gold
			We Three Kings
189	Chapter 28	The Prodigal Son	Once a Brother, Always a Brother (s-a)
		Forgiveness	*Amazing Grace* (s-a)
195	Chapter 29	Jesus and Zacchaeus	Love Begins with Giving (s-a)
		Friendship and Forgiveness	

	PART SEVEN Non-Bible Stories for Special Occasions		Songs
203	Introduction		
205	Chapter 30	Hanukkah Importance of Faith	*Hanukkah, Oh Hanukkah* (s-a)
211	Chapter 31	Martin Luther King Jr. Celebrations The Ice Cream Shop	*Amazing Grace* (s-a) *We Shall Overcome*
		The Land of Color Curves	Curve Song Work a Little Bit (s-a)
223	Chapter 32	Saint Francis Based on the Life of Saint Francis	Love Begins with Giving (s-a) I Heard the Birds Sing

PART EIGHT The Songbook

233 Introduction

237 Sing-along Songs

ACKNOWLEDGMENTS

I want to acknowledge The Episcopal School in the City of New York (with during my twenty-plus years tenure, Directors Dick Davis, Carole Lembo, Cheryl Kelly, and presently Judith Blanton) where all this work began and continues, and which awarded me a summer writing grant to complete this manuscript. In particular, I want to thank my colleagues at Episcopal, Christopher Minarich and Karen Diaz (Directors of Music and Creative Movement respectively) who musically accompany every chapel and are always ready to try new ideas and offer superb suggestions to make the chapels more meaningful for the children. When former director Cheryl Kelly led the chapel gatherings, our weekly meetings allowed my work with story-telling to become integrated into the stories. Present director Judith Blanton invited me to take the helm and continues to support my leading of songs and stories by discussing the story selection, welcoming the families, and placing the children's artwork on the felt board to accompany the stories.

The teachers at Episcopal must also be applauded for their willingness to join the "Band," hand out songbooks, and guide the art-making. A number of our teachers have also enriched the whole process with their solo singing of special songs and with their observations and suggestions through the years.

I also want to acknowledge the support of Peter Cheney and the National Association of Episcopal Schools who have supported this work and provided numerous opportunities to share it with other schools. My literary agent, Michele Rubin with Writers House, deserves kudos for her friendship and ongoing support of my writing work. Finally I want to give a special thanks to Betsy Hooper who offered invaluable suggestions regarding the content and presentation of the material.

FOREWORD

In the fall of 1998, just a few months after beginning my work with the National Association of Episcopal Schools, I made a formal visit to The Episcopal School in the City of New York, the exemplary early childhood center where Bill Gordh serves as Director of Expressive Arts. A friend and parish youth director from Arizona had seen Bill perform at the annual White House Easter Egg Roll and had gotten to know Bill and his work. She told me, "You simply must visit Bill at his school in New York and witness the chapel services that he conducts with the school's director, Cheryl Kelly. He is incredible!" And so I made an appointment with Bill and Cheryl and made my way to their school.

In my thirty-two years of formal ministry with Episcopal schools and congregations I can count on one hand the number of people that I have worked with, who truly "get" how to lead and assist young children in corporate worship. It looks easy from a distance but it is actually extremely challenging to do effectively. One reason is that our culture does not reward it: almost all who make their vocation in any area of early childhood education are undervalued and undercompensated. The "real" work—as the marketplace rewards it—is with adults, and the food chain descends from there. "Many are called, but few respond"—to put a twist on a well-known saying of Jesus.

My experience that first day with Bill was genuinely exciting. At last, I had found a model I had been searching for, one that might be summarized and made adaptable for early childhood education programs and congregations throughout the church. The ideal would be to create clones of Bill himself and to distribute "him" around the country. I write only partly in jest because Bill is really *that* good. The older I get the more in awe I am of genuine excellence, and one nods in respect wherever it is discovered. Bill is that good, but even more important in my mind is his devotion to the lives and spiritual formation of young children.

After that first visit to Episcopal, my first instinct was to encourage early childhood education leaders to visit Episcopal and witness Bill at work, and also to make Bill available through NAES's conferences, both national and regional. That we have done—and the responses have been predictably enthusiastic. Likewise, Bill has been willing to serve as a consultant to individual schools, and to groups of schools and their leaders; and he now offers a course at the General Theological Seminary in New York on story-telling and music for worship with young children—an elective open to seminarians and the general public.

It also became clear to Bill, and then in conversation with my late colleague Jonathan Glass and with me, that the best way to share his magic and insights is through a book, whereby he could demonstrate how actually to adapt biblical stories and music for worship with the young—worship that respects them and their incredible joy and faith through conscious attunement to their needs and levels of development as human beings.

Bill set to work and over two or three summers created the wonderful work that you are about to read and incorporate into your own ministry with children. I am deeply grateful to Bill for his friendship, for his passion for the young and for his teaching. He has been wonderfully patient through a long process to find a publisher. It has been worth the wait: Frank Tedeschi, the Vice President and Executive Editor at Church Publishing Incorporated, took Bill and this project under his wing, and at last you now hold the finished product.

Peter G. Cheney
Retired Executive Director, National Association of Episcopal Schools
Interim Headmaster, St. Richard's School, Indianapolis
September 2007

AUTHOR'S PREFACE

Many questions arise when creating a successful children's chapel. Where shall it be held? Will all the children attend or only some? How often shall we meet? Will one chapel gather work for all the children or should we plan more? How long should the chapel be? Shall we invite the parents? Trying to answer these questions leads us to consider the nature of the chapel itself. What will occur at the chapel? Shall we sing? What songs? Will there be a story or stories? What stories? How long should they be? Interestingly, all these questions and answers interact with each other. The answer to one may help determine the response to another, or it may open up a whole other group of questions. The questions and answers are part of this ongoing process. The answers are not definitive, nor should they be. We try things and learn from what results. Groups change. Colleagues bring different skills and talents. These and many other factors continue to affect our choices.

This book came about as a result of many years helping develop the chapel program at The Episcopal School in the City of New York. In 1998, Peter Cheney, Executive Director of NAES (National Association of Episcopal Schools) visited one of our chapels and was excited about the work we were (and are) doing. As we began collaborating on workshops about developing chapels for young children, we found many people were interested in what we have discovered in creating a dynamic chapel program. For the fall semester 2007 a course was added in "Creating a Childhood Chapel" at the General Theological Seminary taught by the author. This work keeps evolving and we hope our discoveries will be helpful to you.

At The Episcopal School, children attend chapel once a week; we have a total of four services each week, divided by age groups (three-year-olds and four-year-olds). The story content is adapted to suit the developmental levels of the young listeners. Parents are expected to attend with their children, which creates both opportunities and specific challenges. The school Board of Directors decided that the Bible should be the source for most of the stories shared. These tales are complex and often confusing to young children, yet the majority of "Bible Stories for Children" books available seem simplistic rather than simple and often offer poorly crafted stories. This is a disservice to the Bible and to the minds of young children. Having successfully developed a storytelling program for young children in which I have taken folktales from around the world and retold them incorporating rhymes, rhythms, simple vocabulary, and musical refrains, I began to apply these ideas to Bible stories.

Stories from the Bible are rich with meaning; the challenge became finding and illuminating themes that would resonate with the children and support the mission of the school. These topics include children working together, helping each other, learning empathy, sharing, being a good neighbor, and beginning to see the importance of making the world a better place for all to live in. The Bible stories retold in this book are the result of exploring these stories and then telling them many times, allowing them to change in response to the listening children. It has been an amazing experience, and I believe that you will find these "versions" of the stories helpful in your work.

While I hope you find the stories included beautifully rendered, I present them here for you to use as the basis for your own work, not as pieces to memorize. Although you can create a significant experience for children by reading these stories aloud, for more meaningful interaction, retell these stories yourself. This will allow your knowledge of the children in front of you to affect the flow and energy of your presentations. I have written these stories down after sharing them many times, but they continue to change as the children before me provide different circumstances for me to understand the stories and how they can be most effective. I include tips for each story to help you feel comfortable in your own retelling.

The Organization of the Book

PART ONE: CREATING THE FRAMEWORK FOR CHAPEL

This section is a practical guide to deciding how you wish your program to work, from the importance of telling stories to the length of the service and setting up a space for chapel. I also discuss creating a songbook for non- and early readers and incorporating the children's artwork. By the end of Part One, you should be ready to make your own choices about building your chapel program.

PARTS TWO - SIX: THE BIBLE STORIES ORGANIZED BY THEMES

The theme is often the basis of the story choice for a particular chapel, so the stories are grouped accordingly. The themes are **Stories of Self; Stories of Family and Friends; Stories of Faith, New Life, and Celebration; Stories of the Value of All Living Things; and Stories of Giving and Forgiving.** Each section has a number of Bible stories in it; each Bible story is for a distinct chapel and has its own chapter in the book. However, not surprisingly a number of the stories support more than one theme. Each chapter includes:

- A brief introduction to the story and the rationale for choices made regarding the telling of the story.
- Suggestion for spoken introduction at chapel before telling the story.
- The Story
- Suggestion for what to say following the story to relate the chapel time to life at school.
- Story-telling tips specific to the story.
- Musical notation and lyrics for story refrain.
- Description of artwork created by children to accompany story.
- Skeleton of story to guide retelling.

PART SEVEN: SOME SPECIAL NON-BIBLE STORIES FOR CHAPEL

This section includes a Hanukkah story, a story based on the life of St. Francis and two stories that can be used in conjunction with Martin Luther King Day. These subjects are common in chapel programs and thus are included here. There is also a brief discussion of using folktales from around the world to further support the themes explored in chapel.

PART EIGHT: THE SONGBOOK

Part Eight includes thematic songs that can be used before the story in a group sing-along and following the story to continue the theme of the chapel. I wrote the songs presented in this section (other than "A Snake named LaRue") especially to support the goals of the chapel program. I also suggest traditional songs and songs written by others that can be considered for your songbook.

This book is the culmination of years of working with young children and amazing material. We have road-tested these ideas, and I hope that they will serve you well in your work with young children.

part 1

CREATING THE FRAMEWORK FOR CHAPEL

chapter 1

SETTING UP CHAPEL

Where Shall We Have Chapel?

Keep it simple! The space we use for chapel is a carpeted room in the basement of the school. At one end are a simple altar, a piano, an easel with felt board, and a few stools for musicians and song leader. Behind the altar is a large woven wall hanging created years ago by school parents that has simple images from Bible stories. There are no chairs in the room. Everyone sits on the carpet facing the altar. There are built-in benches on either side of the front half of the room. The other half of the room's walls house books on shelves for the library. When the benches were installed, we thought perhaps some of the families would sit on them for chapel. As we considered it further, the fact that only a small number could sit on the benches led us to decide that everyone (other than a grandparent or very pregnant mom) would continue in our tradition of children and parents sitting together on the floor. Our school is in New York City and though many parents are on their way to work, they happily join the others in their work clothes (generally business suits) with child in lap sitting together on the rug. The room is simple and handled simply, and it serves us well.

Some schools use the sanctuary of the church. Others use an auditorium, a gymnasium, or a classroom. Each situation creates its own benefits and challenges. Wherever your chapel is held, the size of the space and the size of the children should be taken into consideration. What might at first glance look perfect to an adult may not be the right circumstance for a young child. For example, sitting in pews can make children feel isolated from the others in their class. Many schools solve this by having everyone gather in the chancel, or by having the children gather in the chancel while parents sit in the pews. Some schools go ahead and use the sanctuary without considering whether another available space in the building might actually serve their purposes better. What at first might seem like a terrible choice (like a carpeted room in a basement!) might actually offer just what you need – a simple space to gather with children.

Choosing a setting with few visual or sound distractions (or smells for that matter) will help the children stay focused on the story and songs and being together. When there are fewer potential distractions, you can have fewer rules to control the behavior. The children become engaged in the story and "follow the rules" without being told. A simple setting is a good place to start.

Who Will Attend?

The immediate answer to this question is simple: Children. Of course the chapels are for children and therefore children will attend, but how many and when? How about parents? If the school has a preschool, kindergarten, and lower grades, do all the students attend together? The answer to all these questions is: "It depends." It depends on your particular circumstances.

Our school is devoted to early childhood, with over two hundred preschoolers attending. The youngest begin at two-plus and the oldest are five when they leave. We have decided that our chapels will *not* include our youngest children. The behavioral expectations would not be fair and the stories are too complex. This is not to say that there are no stories in this book appropriate for such young children. Some are and can be shared with the youngest children, with care and in a very small group. At our school the children begin chapel in the fall when they are three. Our school has morning and afternoon sessions, so we have chapels for both sessions. We have three classes of three-year-olds and three classes of four-year-olds in each session, so we have a discrete chapel for each of these age groups. On Wednesday, we have chapel for fours and on Thursday for threes. The children get to share the experience with two other classes of children as well as with their parents. This provides them a larger group experience and makes them more aware of and a part of the whole school. Thursday chapel is for the younger group because it gives the children several days in school each week before the chapel gathering with a large group. Additionally, we have told the story already for the Wednesday fours' group so the story can more easily be tailored for the younger listeners.

The size of many early-childhood (including kindergarten) schools makes one chapel for the whole group the right choice. In a school with Pre-K through elementary, you probably will want to group the Pre-K and kindergarten (and possibly first) together, with a separate chapel program for second to fifth grades. For special occasions, if you have the space, it's nice to have the whole school gather together.

PARENTS ATTEND

We invite the parents to bring their children and stay for chapel each week. In fact, it is assumed (and expected) that at least one parent will attend chapel each week. This is *our community time together*, and by the end of the year, the parents have spent the majority of *their* time at school attending chapel with their children. Many parents remark that at first they were not keen on coming to chapel but soon grew to enjoy it. When their children have moved on to another school, many, many parents have let us know how they miss the weekly gatherings. The fact that the parents attend chapel dictates when our chapels take place—at the beginning of the session (in our case 8:30 a.m. and 12:30 p.m.). The parents sit with their children on the floor in the chapel. On occasion a parent is unable to attend. In this circumstance, a grandparent, relative, adult family friend, or caregiver is welcomed.

Why Children Sit with Parents

At many gatherings with children and parents present, I have seen the children sitting together at the front with the parents gathered in the back. The reasoning behind this is that the event is really for children and this seating arrangement makes them the focus. Additionally, it keeps the seated grown-ups from blocking the sight lines for the children. These seem like very good reasons. However, what often happens is this: because the parents are gathered in the back with the focus on the children, they forget that they are still in the same space and often talk with each other. With the added noise from the back, the children are less attentive. However, the most important reason for seating parents with their children is so that parent and child *share the chapel experience.* Singing together and hearing a story that can later be discussed is a shared experience profoundly different from one where the children and grown-ups are seated separately (especially in early childhood).

Some parents bring a younger sibling with the child who is attending chapel. The younger child is welcomed as long as the chapel remains relatively peaceful. On occasion, a parent might leave the room with a crying baby. We wait patiently when this occurs. Sometimes the parent chooses to leave the younger one home with a caregiver. The younger siblings are generally engaged by these stories and the warmth of sitting with family, and they look forward to the time when they will attend our school and each can say "my" chapel.

Many childhood chapel programs do not include the parents. Clearly it is not imperative, but it is central to our gatherings. If your chapels do not include the parents, before revamping your whole program or rejecting the entire idea, consider trying out family chapels on several occasions during the year. At the end of the year, you will have a clearer idea what direction you wish to follow.

How Often Should We Have Chapel?

We have chapel once a week for the school year. This seems just right as the children grow accustomed to and excited about the weekly gathering. The children come to chapel with their parents at the beginning of the session. In this way it is similar to the child's experience of the other days—i.e., entering school with a parent but with a bonus. The parent gets to stay for a half hour with the child. Following chapel the parent walks the child to the classroom and says good-bye at the classroom door like the other days.

How Long Should It Be?

We have found that a half-hour program is perfect. Our time is divided between singing together and listening to a story. Generally we sing for ten or fifteen minutes at the beginning of the chapel. The vast majority arrive for the first sing-along song, but this set-up allows for children with a parent to arrive during the singing. We then tell the story. Depending on the story, this segment lasts from five to fifteen minutes, though most of the stories presented in this book can be told in about ten to twelve minutes. We close with a theme-related sing-along. Half an hour is a good length of time for chapel through second grade.

How Will Children Come and Go?

At many schools where the parents are not a part of the equation, the children are brought with their classes, sit with their group, and leave with their teachers. This allows for the chapel to be held at a convenient time for all the classes.

Having parents at chapel has many benefits, but with young children, saying good-bye is a bit more of a challenge. These children have gotten used to saying good-bye to their parents at the classroom door and getting on with their school day. For a child to sit and sing and listen to a story at school with a parent is very special, but separating can be difficult. At our school, for years the parents said good-bye to the children in the chapel space and the young children gathered with their teachers to return to the classroom. This often resulted in at least one crying child or one still clinging to a parent's leg. This will happen on occasion no matter what you do. However, we have found that by having the parents walk with their children to the classroom following chapel, the children fall into a known routine—saying good-bye at the classroom door. It has made a huge difference. Many of the discoveries we have made seem obvious once they are in place, but not until then. So we continue to observe the children and discuss any problems to see if we can adjust to make the experience more meaningful.

The Format

EARLY CHILDHOOD

Our chapels consist of singing and sharing a story. Each chapel we begin by singing songs from our *Chapel Songbook*. Following a period of singing (around ten minutes), the school's director joins us and we announce, "Page one!" Page one provides the lyrics to the song ("Now Is the Time") we sing at every chapel before the story. The director then welcomes everyone, makes a brief comment about the day's story, and acknowledges the group that made the artwork that will accompany the story.

The story is then told. Following the story, the director comments on how it relates to life at school. Then she announces the name and page number of the thematically selected sing-along song. After the entire group sings the song, the director directs the families to accompany their children to their classrooms.

Prayer: Many chapel programs close their gatherings with a prayer. Although we refer to prayer in the stories, the content of the prayers is generally left to the imagination of the listeners. Our school welcomes a range of families to our chapels, and we feel that the use of prayers is a personal choice for them—to be followed at home and their church. In Sunday schools, leaders may wish to use a prayer at the end of the story, before or after a song. There is an opportunity here to use the children's reflections on the story to create a prayer for the group.

ELEMENTARY

The format offered above is excellent for very young children. This basic outline can be expanded upon for older children (first to fifth grades). Singing together is welcome with any age group, and with older children you can sing more verses of songs as well as ones with more complicated music. Often a class will prepare a special song to open or close a chapel. You can expand the story by including the students as singers or actors (or narrators). The refrains included in this book are in good keys for young singers. Some schools also have students read a passage from the Bible to accompany the story. At Saint Mark's School in Altadena, California, students light and extinguish the candles on the altar followed by a moment of silence to appreciate the flame (or smoke). Often the chapel in elementary grades is also a time for announcements. Trinity School in New York City uses chapel as an opportunity to share anecdotes of students helping someone. Actively involving the children in the chapel gatherings should be a focus of elementary chapels.

The Stories

Stories are the centerpiece of our chapel program. There are many excellent stories that can be used for a chapel gathering. Picture books, folktales, personal stories and Bible stories can all contribute to a vibrant program. Picture books for young children offer a story they can revisit on their own or with others. Folktales demonstrate to children that we learn from many cultures. Personal stories remind children that everyone has experiences in common and that we learn from events in others' lives. Bible stories offer a wealth and depth of story that is central to our culture. As stated in the Author's Preface, the majority of this book is devoted to the telling of Bible stories. Each biblical story in this collection has been examined for what it offers in meaning, in story shape, and in how it can be retold using my knowledge of young children and stories to make a truly meaningful and memorable tale for young listeners.

WHY TELL STORIES?

The Bible stories in this book were told many times before they were written down. The fact that they have been written down does not mean that they are now in a definitive form. In fact when I tell them, they continue to change. They change because of the listeners. Some groups need to hear a phrase repeated, and you can see that in their eyes or in their restlessness. Some groups of children require a more energetic telling, while others like a quieter delivery. It is true that you can be responsive to your listeners when you are reading, but it is easier for you and more meaningful to them if the story is told, not recited word for word. Then it exists in the space shared by you and your listeners. It offers you the opportunity to find the phrase that can be repeated by the children, allowing them to become a storyteller too and help you tell the story. It is in the moment of the telling that you can keep active the interface of teller/listener in most meaningful ways. This is not something that will happen immediately, but will accumulate over many sessions. This does not mean that the first times will not be meaningful! They will, for the children sense the immediacy and presence of a story told. As you become comfortable you will notice more ways of adjusting your stories to your listeners. Following each story in this collection, you will find "Story-telling Tips." They are specific to each story, while offering ideas that will accumulate with the others as you use them. To summarize and clarify:

WHAT TELLING A STORY OFFERS TO THE CHAPEL EXPERIENCE

- Telling a story allows the relationship to be exclusively between you and the children listeners, rather than having a book as intermediary. Even if you know the words in a book, you will turn to it as you are reading, breaking into your relationship with your young listeners.
- Telling the story allows you to be extremely responsive to the children and provides the opportunity to alter the way you're telling the story as you go. You will use different words different times. This keeps it fresh and in the moment. Memorizing a story word for word is very time-consuming and tends to make you focus on trying to remember the words rather than on telling the story. You will find the "Story Skeletons" at the end of each story helpful for retelling rather than memorizing.
- Children sense the "magic" of a story being told, seeing it as a privilege and giving it attention that they don't when they know they can pick up the book later and look at it.
- It is hard to deviate from the text of a written story even if you sense that something should be altered. Telling a story is specific to the moment in which it is told.

GETTING COMFORTABLE TELLING STORIES (START SLOWLY!)

Having read the section above, you may agree with the importance of telling the stories but may still feel uncomfortable trying it. Here are some ideas to guide you.

When telling stories, use your own vocabulary and develop your own personal style. This allows the children listeners to feel at home because it is you personally telling them the stories!

APPROACHING TELLING A STORY

- Select a story according to the theme you wish to explore/present in your chapel. Read through the story. Read it over a few times. Do *not* try to memorize it, but rather begin to remember how the story moves—i.e., the plot. If there are certain phrases in the story that you really love, go back and read them a few more times so they become yours. Try to retell the story using the story skeleton offered at the end of the chapter. Are there more cues than you need? Mark through them. Are there things missing that you loved in the written story? Add them. Are there other aspects from your own reading of the story in the Bible that are important to you? Add them to your skeleton. The story is becoming your story now, and by using your own words and expressions, the children will be more responsive.
- **Using the Skeletons** There is a story skeleton at the end of each chapter for the story that is presented. It offers the basic plot of the story. You can use it as a reference when you practice retelling the story. You can use the skeleton when you retell the story in chapel. If you do use it, don't hide it. Place it in front of you where the listeners know that you are using it. If later a child asks you, you can simply say that it helps you remember the story. This in turn shows the child that one develops strategies to accomplish something she or he wishes to do.
- **For Elementary** The skeleton can also be very helpful for devising a "staged" version of one of the stories. The skeleton becomes the base for which the children create dialogue. Again as with telling the story, the dialogue does not need to be memorized; instead, children should know the idea of what is being said. This keeps the young actors alert and present to the story that they are helping to tell. Their attention then is on the story instead of on memorizing what they are supposed to say.

MUSIC AND CHAPEL

Music is central to the chapel program. It welcomes everyone as we begin with singing songs from the songbook. The music continues its support by providing an underscore for the stories and in the many refrains that are included within the tales. Each gathering closes with a final song in support of the theme of the particular chapel.

When the child and parent walk into chapel, a teacher offers them a songbook. Then they find a place on the carpet to sit. The "band" is sitting up front ready to sing. Sometimes we will sing a song as the families enter. Other times we wait for the first request. The children look through the songbook to find a song they want to sing. They hold up their books to show us what they have chosen. We select one of the songs, give everyone time to find it (fun for the children and helpful for the parents) and we all sing together. When one song has been sung, we look around again at the upraised books and select another song. We choose a number of children each session and try for a range of songs as well. By the end of the school year, everyone who wants to will have suggested a song. Thus our sing-along is led by the children's choices of songs. In order for the children to become familiar with all the songs in the book, we will also select and announce the less familiar songs during the sing-along time. This same approach will work well in weekly Sunday school classes.

Secondly, music is used as an integral part of the story-telling. There are simple refrains that occur within many of the stories that help support its theme and make it a more memorable event for the listeners. The refrains also act as structural supports for the tale that help the children stay with the story. At our chapels, we are fortunate to have a group of musicians accompanying the stories. This adds excitement to the event. Many different instruments can be used to enhance a story, from wood blocks to cello. You can build your chapel's story-sound with the instruments that you and your colleagues can play. Often there are parent musicians who will happily be part of your program. We have had parents sing, play cello, saxophone, accordion, piano, electric guitar, and harmonica. These were great additions to the chapel and provided extra fun for the children.

HOW WE ORGANIZED OUR SONGBOOK

Our songbook is divided into five sections that reflect the themes of our chapels: "Bible Story Songs," "Sharing and Caring," "Working and Working," "You and Me," and "Holiday Songs." Each section is printed on a different color paper to help the children (nonreaders) notice the different sections and to entice them to look through the whole book when searching for a song to suggest. Since these children are pre-readers, there are simple illustrations accompanying each song so they recognize the song and their parents have the lyrics to join in on the singing. There is only one song on each page so it is clear which song has been chosen. Each page is numbered three ways: The numeral (1, 2, 3), the word (one, two, three), and simple repeated symbols (x, xx, xxx) corresponding with the number. All these elements make the book more meaningful to the children and support the development of early literacy. We sometimes say, "Choose a color and then look in that section. Find the picture you like and we'll sing the song."

CHOOSING SONGS FOR YOUR SONGBOOK

Part Eight offers original songs (lyrics and musical notation) that support the themes of the chapel stories and suggestions for other songs that are generally well-known and simple to track down. The contents of your songbook should evolve to reflect the families that make up your school or Sunday school, as well as the larger community. If there are songs that are already popular at your school or Sunday school, include them. These already-favorite songs become an immediate invitation to the children to be part of the singing at chapel. For instance, the song "She'll Be Coming Round the Mountain" is not a likely choice for a chapel songbook. However, if it's a song the children all love singing, then it's worth considering. For that matter, the song celebrates a family getting together; and when it's sung at a chapel it will bring out this meaning. The songs presented in this book will not be familiar; you will want to mix them in with a group of songs the children and families already know. These new songs were inspired by the stories, and so once you know them, you will see how well they go with the chapel. Over time, you can incorporate more of them. The chapel songbook is an ongoing process.

- **The Sing–Along** Singing together is central to the school-as-community experience. Singing songs that celebrate the shared hopes and dreams for world fellowship make the children part of the process. By singing songs together, they feel the strength of this community. Singing with family at chapel further enriches this experience for a young child.
- **Leading the Sing-Along** Having children help choose the songs makes the chapel communal and moves them toward joining the singing. If you play an instrument, have someone up front with you to hold up the songbook to show which song to sing.

  You or your fellow singer up front should use specific gestures with the songs whenever possible. Gestures provide children with a physical relationship to the music and help them remember the sequence of the song. In traditional Bible songs like "Arkie, Arkie", you can demonstrate the building of the ark by tapping your fists like a hammer and showing rain with wiggly fingers. Create physical accompaniment to other songs with very simple hand movements.

- **How Long Should the Songs Be?** A song like "Arkie, Arkie" has six verses. This is a long song for young singers but, because of its story line and added gestures, the children remember it. With more complicated songs, you may want to sing one verse and the chorus, perhaps beginning with the chorus so that you sing it twice. For elementary-age children, you can sing full songs. Sometimes you will want to sing longer songs because of the content, even if the children cannot sing along for the whole tune. By the end of the year, they will probably know them as well.
- **Musical Range of Songs** For young children (3–5 years), it is best to sing songs that are within their range (Middle-C–A), though it is good for them to listen to songs with greater ranges. The songs in the song section of this book are written in keys to make them best for young singers. It should be noted that some children have a much wider range at a very young age and others less.

THE MUSICIANS FOR CHAPEL

We are very fortunate at our school to have several musicians who regularly participate in chapel. They accompany the sing-along before and after the story as well as play along as the tale is told. We have banjo (or guitar), another guitar, violin, and a drum (djembe). Additionally, each week there are two classroom teachers who join "the band" for chapel. The teachers take turns throughout the year. One classroom teacher joins us as a singer who holds up the songbook page to show what song we will sing and leads the gestures that accompany the songs. Another teacher adds to the band's sound as a percussionist. We discuss the possible percussion choices from a variety of instruments (claves, ratchet, eggs, castanets, etc.) to go along with our story. If there are specific cues, we get together a few minutes early and go over them. Everyone has fun being in the band, and it's great for the children to see their teachers up front being part of the chapel gathering.

Simple accompaniment can be very effective. The "shaky–eggs" that are egg-shaped rattles with tiny beads inside give a wonderful sound to accompany singing or special places in a story. Rhythm sticks, small bells, and tambourines are all easy-to-play and exciting additions to the sounds in chapel. The easy-yet-attentive playing is also something the young children will watch and hear and be eager to try in the classroom.

All these musicians are not necessary to assure an exhilarating musical experience for the children, but they add to the community feeling. The willingness of "non-musician musicians" to be part of the process is the first and major ingredient. The music will grow as the musicians play more and more together.

ACCOMPANYING STORIES WITH INSTRUMENTS

Most of the stories in our chapel program are accompanied by music. I play the banjo and set up a bed of music on which to tell the story. This generally means using a picking style that repeats with one or two chords in the rhythm that I am going to tell the story. The other musicians (guitar and djembe) solidify this musical bed and help it move along. We have found that if the music stops at dramatic points, everyone's attention is drawn to the silence and they listen intently. We also stop the music when one of the characters speaks. It is good to change the rhythm and style of play as the story progresses so that the music continually activates the story rather than becoming a drone. The guest musician can add fun rhythmical touches to the story with the percussion instruments chosen before chapel. Often the "band" joins in singing the refrain in the story. This process may seem daunting for people who do not consider themselves musicians, but start simply and as you get more comfortable add to the elements of the accompaniment.

CHILDREN'S ART AND CHAPEL

Many children are visual learners, and offering them visual support to the story is important. There are many commercial felt-board Bible story sets available for just such a purpose. We have found something simpler and, I believe, more meaningful. For all our chapels, *children create the artwork.* In our school there are six classes that attend chapel, and we present art created by one of the classes to accompany each story. The classes take turns; the first chapel art assignment goes to the oldest class, the second to the next oldest, and so on. We give a sheet to the teacher with a list of our art needs and a brief retelling of the story to help guide the art-making process. You will find a list of "Art Needs" following each story. These lists are handed out in advance so that the classroom teacher has time to fit the art-making into the classroom schedule.

When the teacher gets the list, she or he decides how and when to proceed. Some teachers share a brief telling of the story before the class makes the artwork. Other classes find it fun to make the artwork and let the children find out what will happen with the characters at chapel. As the children in the classes are different ages and have a range of skills, the teachers offer guidance accordingly. Using artwork from the children of various classes provides an opportunity to have an active interface with the classroom, a regular time when we are all working toward the same event. You will notice in the art list that there are optional pieces named. The reason for this is to make the creation of the art a flexible situation for the teachers. Sometimes the children are very excited and everyone wants to do something. At other times, the teacher is involved with a number of other projects in the classroom, so fulfilling the minimum needs works better. By including the optional on the list, you are acknowledging the realities of the classroom, something the teachers appreciate.

As the year progresses, the teacher can discuss the artwork with the students and its use with the story. For instance, if children make a very tiny animal for a story, the teacher can ask how will it be seen from the back of the chapel space. The students themselves will become more active in noticing effective art in size and color for supporting the stories.

A couple of examples will help show the significance of the children's art at chapel gatherings and in the creation process.

The Creation Story For the creation story, we request distinct artwork to go with each day of the story (except for Day One when we close our eyes for darkness). The development of this artwork allows the children to look around and think about the beauty of the world, of their favorite trees and flowers, sea creatures, bird and land animals, and then to "create" the work that illustrates Creation. For classes that do not make the artwork for a specific story, the teacher might want to go back and let the class create artwork for retelling the story in the classroom.

Blessings for the Baby Jesus The commercial felt-board characters have a very specific look. Children's artwork does not. Therefore the children will provide you with many different ways of presenting the figures of Jesus and the other characters. The children accept the different portrayals, and by having such a range of presentations you are providing a more inclusive view. For example, for the story of the blessing of the baby Jesus by Simeon and Anna, one class made baby Jesus huge and Joseph and Mary very tiny. A few parents smiled or chuckled when the baby was shown, but as we considered what they had done, it was clear the children understood the story in a way that we had not and made that understanding visual: baby Jesus should be the largest figure in the story! This kind of special occurrence can only happen when the children are part of the process.

Children look forward to the chapel that will feature their artwork. They are more attentive. They tell their parents and point out their contributions. As you get used to telling the tales, you can use the specifics of the children's artwork to accentuate an aspect of the story. When children have worked energetically at creating a Popsicle-stick stable and manger, your story can describe Mary looking around and admiring the stable where baby Jesus will be born. You can use the story to support the children's pride in their contribution.

PRACTICING WITH THE ARTWORK

You will want to have the artwork ahead of time. We use a felt board, and the art has rounds of masking tape on the back ready to be placed. Once you have the artwork, go through the story to decide when and where you want to place the art. Placing the artwork will also help you remember the sequence of the story! If there is a lot of art, you will want to see if it can all be on the board at the same time. If it cannot all fit, you need to figure out what is important to stay in place and what can be moved off the board. Some stories call for the art to be moved to different locations on the board during the story. Some stories will guide you to take the art off and then bring it back. For some stories you may want to have some of the artwork already in place. For instance, for "The Parable of the Lost Sheep," in which the little sheep is found behind a rock, you may decide to have the rock (with the lamb hidden behind it) and tree and bush on the board at the beginning at the story. You may find putting up the artwork yourself enhances your telling of the story. I play banjo while telling stories, so our director puts up the artwork. Another possibility is to ask a teacher who guided the creation of the art to be your assistant. There are many effective ways to incorporate the children's work into the story presentation. The children's wonderful art will make almost any choice turn out all right!

In addition to presetting and adding and taking away artwork, an approach that works well for many tales is to introduce a character and keep it up on the board for the whole story. Each new character is introduced and kept on the board as well, so by the end of the story the board ends up illustrating all that occurred. There's not a "correct" way of doing this. In fact you may find that for different stories you approach presenting the art differently, but most likely you will find one or two techniques that support the way you tell stories. You will find what works to accompany the tone of your chapel and your particular style of story-telling. As the presentation of the art becomes the norm for the whole group, the teachers and artwork will also support the evolution of the chapel program.

DISPLAYING ART AFTER THE STORY

We have bulletin boards throughout the school and have begun displaying the chapel art on these boards following the chapels. We place the artwork on boards near the children's classrooms so they can stop by, show their families and enjoy their work, and remember the story they helped tell.

Part One/Chapter One has provided the format and rationale behind the choices made for creating an effective and exciting early-childhood chapel. The remainder of the book provides the content for the chapel gatherings and specific notes on making the particular story meaningful to your listeners.

NOTE TO LEADERS

Each story chapter begins with a title, the story theme, scriptural reference, and sing-along song title. Within the body of the story are the words to the refrains that may be sung or said by the leader. When they appear, the text is set off with a note (♫) icon to make the music spots easy to locate. The actual music appears in the Story Skeleton to encourage the *telling* of the story. The full music is placed when it first occurs, and subsequent repetitions or verses are literally "noted" (♫) only.

There are numerous traditional songs within the stories that are not included in this book but may be found in various other sources or on the Internet. The Table of Contents lists the songs as they appear in each chapter.

Three songs — "A Snake Named LaRue," "Now Is the Time," and "The Very First Christmas" are included in the songbook in Part Eight, but do not occur in the stories. They may be added as needed.

part 2

STORIES OF SELF

chapter 2

CREATION

GENESIS 1:1 – 2:3

A Story about the Joy of Creativity

Sing-along "You've Got Me" (p. 258)

This story presents a wonderful model for the creative process: considering, creating, taking a look at what has been created and feeling satisfied with the results. This is the kind of experience we want the children to have at school. The creation of the artwork for this story provides the children with an opportunity to consider the many wonders that fill the world. They then get to create images of these mountains and animals and trees and flowers to help tell the story.

BEFORE THE STORY

The first chapel story of this year is the first story in the Bible; the story of creation and how everything began. The artwork was created by _______ .

OR

Our first chapel is a story from the Bible. We will begin at the beginning—the beginning of the world—the story of creation. And the artwork is by _______ .

THE STORY

In the very beginning there was nothing at all—nothing! And it was dark—dark, dark, dark. So dark that if you close your eyes as tight as you can, it was darker than that. So dark that if you closed your eyes and sat in your closet, with the closet door shut and a coat over your head, it was darker than that. It was dark all the time. God thought the dark was beautiful, but he wanted something else too. So God said, "Let there be light!"

And there was light and it was glorious. And now there was light and darkness.

And that was day number one. God looked at the light and thought of the darkness and the first day of creation.

And

♫ **It was good, good, good,**
you know it was good!
Now we come to day number two.

On day number two God saw the light and the dark, but he wanted more than that. So God made the sky and clouds. He blew the puffy clouds across the sky. All day long he watched the clouds. They were beautiful and God smiled. At the end of the day, God looked at his work.

♫ **It was good, good, good,**
you know it was good!
Now we come to day number three.

On day number three, God gazed down at the earth. It was just flat empty land, and God wanted to put some thing on the earth. So God made mountains rise into the sky and sprinkled some snow on their peaks. In those mountains God dug caves. Then God created rivers to flow across the land. God liked the rivers and decided to make other things with water. So he made streams and lakes and ponds and springs and, of course, the ocean. On the land God made trees grow, and grass and bushes and beautiful flowers all across the fields. The earth was looking beautiful!

At the end of the day, God looked at his work.

♫ **It was good, good, good,**
you know it was good!
Now we come to day number four.

On day number four, God was watching the clouds moving across the sky. There was daylight but nothing to give out the light. So God made the sun. It was big and shining and warm — just right for the daytime, but way too bright for night. So for nighttime God created the moon and the twinkling stars. Now the sky looked fine.

At the end of the day, God looked at his work.

♫ **It was good, good, good,**
you know it was good!
Now we come to day number five.

On day number five, God took a look at the ocean and the lakes and the streams and decided that it would be nice to have things live there. So on day number five, God made the water creatures. He made goldfish and catfish and tuna and sharks. He made whales and sea stars and anemones too. He made dolphins and sting rays and parrot fish and guppies, lobsters and crabs and octopus and loads more.

Then God looked at the sky and decided he would do the same idea in the sky, but these creatures would fly. So on day number five, God made the birds. He made robins and blue jays and finches and black birds. He made hummingbirds and parrots and hoot-hoot owls. He made eagles and hawks and falcons and condors. All sizes and colors, the birds flitted across the sky.

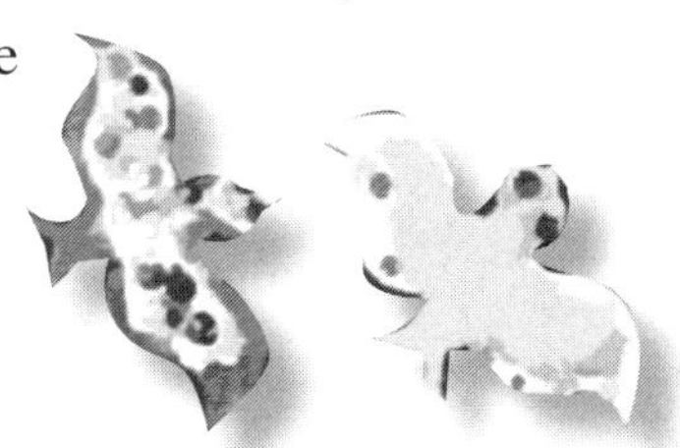

At the end of the day, God looked at his work.

♫ **It was good, good, good,**
you know it was good!
Now we come to day number six.

Now God looked around and was pleased with all the creatures in the sea and sky. He looked in the forest though, and it was quiet. He thought, "There should be animals on the land too." So that's what he did on day number six. He made the land animals. He made dogs and cats and mice. He created kangaroos and lions and tigers; God made raccoons and beavers and coyotes and foxes and wolves and lizards and gorillas and koala bears. He made animals to live on the desert and in caves and in the jungles and across the plains. Big and small, runners and jumpers, God created all the animals that live on the ground on day number six.

God looked around and thought, "I'm going to need some help taking care of this world." So at the end of the sixth day, God created the first two people, man and woman. He named them Adam and Eve. God watched them as they gazed with amazement at the beautiful world. God spoke to Adam and Eve. "It is your job to take care of yourselves and the whole world," he said. "You have each other, and any time you need me, you've got me. You are loved, my friends, and you will always be loved, for the love of God goes on and on and on forever."

At the end of the day, God looked at his work.

♫ **It was good, good, good,**
you know it was good!
Now we come to day number seven.

God had done a lot of work in those six days, and the world was ready for life to continue. But now it was time to rest. And during his rest, God thought about the first week of the world—how on day number one, he made the light, and day number two the sky and the clouds. He thought of day number three and the mountains and streams and flowers and trees. He remembered day number four and the sun and moon and stars. God considered day number five and the creatures in the water and the sky. Then God thought of day number six and all the land creatures and the first woman and man who would help take care of the world. He thought about all that had happened. God was pleased and knew it was important to take time to rest and think about things. At the end of day number seven God looked at all that was created.

♫ **It was good, good, good,**
you know it was good!

AFTER THE STORY

So here at _________we do lots of things; all of us working together and playing and creating. And when you get home, when your parents ask, "How was your day?" I hope you will say,

"It was good, good, good,
you know it was good!"

Now we'll all sing, "You've Got Me."

STORY-TELLING TIPS

- You might speak the "good, good, good" chorus the first time so the children hear the words before they hear words and music.
- Allow the children's artwork to affect your descriptions of the daily creations.

ART NEEDS

- Numbers 1–7
- Some visuals for each day except light and dark for day #1

On day #1 No art for day #1 except the number 1

God made light and dark—night and day.

On day #2

God made sky and clouds.

On day #3

God made rivers, mountains, caves, lakes, flowers, trees, grass.

On day #4

God made sun and moon and stars.

On day #5

God made sea creatures and flying creatures.

On day #6

God made land animals and then woman and man.

On day #7

Rest.

STORY SKELETON

- In the beginning there was darkness.
- Day Number One God made the light.

It Was Good!

(Creation Story)

Bill Gordh

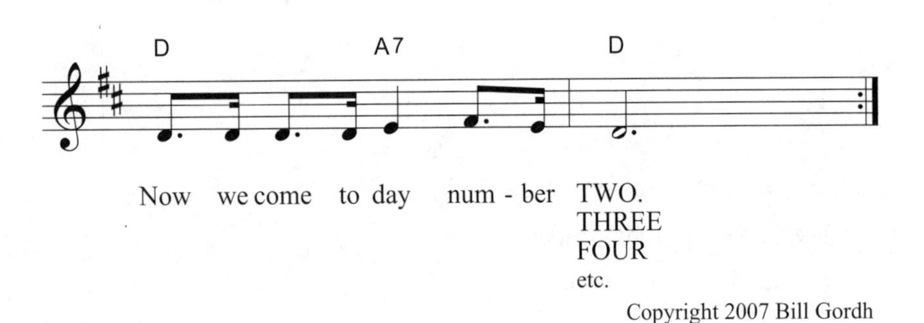

- Day Number Two God made the sky and clouds.

♫

- Day Number Three God made the mountains and the sea—the physical world.

♫

- Day Number Four God made the sun, moon, and stars.

♫

- Day Number Five God made the sea and air creatures.

♫

- Day Number Six God made the land animals and at the end of day woman and man.

♫

- Day Number Seven God rested and thought about the first week of the world.
- Recount what was made.

♫

chapter 3

THE GARDEN OF EDEN
GENESIS 2:15 – 3:24

A Story about Consequences and Learning from Mistakes

Sing-along "In My Garden" (p. 244-245)

In presenting the story of the Garden of Eden, a number of elements seem crucial for young children. These include: the beauty of the garden, the reality of temptation, the admission of making a mistake, the realization and acceptance of resulting consequences, and the realization that the love of God does not disappear as a result of the mistake. The story can also lead to a discussion about our responsibility for taking care of our environment and each other. In the following telling, Adam and Eve are shown making choices, not just obeying or disobeying. Thus God says, "If you *choose* to taste the apple, you will have to leave the garden" rather than "If you *disobey me*, you will have to leave the garden." The decision-making is within the person rather than in reaction to God.

Two possible ways to end the story are included. One stays in the Bible with Adam and Eve. The other brings the story into the present and our lives. How your program works will help determine which will be more appropriate for you.

BEFORE THE STORY

Today's story is again from the Bible. It's about the first two people, Adam and Eve and their life in the Garden of Eden. The artwork is by ______ .

THE STORY

Towards the end of the sixth day, God created the first two people, Adam and Eve. They asked God where they were going to live. God answered, "I have created a very beautiful place just for you. It is the Garden of Eden." God showed them around the garden. He showed them the flowers and the bushes and the grass and waterfalls and streams. He pointed out bunnies and deer and monkeys and kangaroos. He showed them birds of all colors and sizes. God spoke to them as he showed them around, "You will always have plenty of food here, and you will never be cold. This will be your home."

Adam and Eve walked about. They were amazed at the beauty of the garden where they would live. "We love this place!" they exclaimed. They stopped in front of the apple tree. It had a beautiful apple hanging from a branch. "Can we taste that apple?" they asked.

God responded, "Well, that's the one thing you can't do. You cannot taste that apple. You can play and sing and laugh and do all the things you love in this garden, but you can not taste that apple." Adam and Eve looked at the apple, and then they asked God, "What if we do?" "Well," said God, "if you choose to taste the apple you will have to leave the garden."

Adam and Eve thought about what God had told them and said, "Well, if we can play and dance, go swimming, have the food we need and always be warm, that is plenty. We certainly don't need to taste the apple."

And so life went on in the Garden of Eden, and Adam and Eve had a very nice life. They named all the animals. They made up songs. They laughed and ran and jumped and lay on the soft grass at night and counted the stars. AND every day at just about the same time, they wound up standing in front of the apple tree gazing at the apple. It looked delicious, and each day the apple seemed better than the day before! But they always looked at each other and shook their heads and said, "No. No, no, no, no, no! We are not going to taste that apple. We do not want to leave the garden!" Then they turned their backs to the apple tree and walked quickly away.

UNTIL

One day a sneaky snake slithered up the apple tree and waited in the branches for Adam and Eve to come by. Soon the two stopped in front of the tree and once again gazed at the apple. They did not see the snake. After a few moments they looked at each other and shook their heads. Adam and Eve said, "No. No, no, no, no, no! We are not going to taste that apple. We do not want to leave the garden!" Then they turned their backs to the apple tree and started to walk away. The snake stuck its head out from the leaves and sang out

♫ **Hsss, Hsss Would you like to take a bite?**
Hsss, Hsss Would you like to take a bite?
Yes?!

Adam and Eve looked at the snake and sang out

♫ **"No! No, no, no, no, no."**

The snake called out again

♫ **Hsss, Hsss Would you like to take a bite?**
Hsss, Hsss Would you like to take a bite?
Yes?!

Adam and Eve shook their heads and sang out

♫ **"No! No, no, no, no, no."**

The snake suggested, "It'll taste so delicious."

"No!"

"It'll taste mighty sweet.."

"No!"

"Yummy in the tummy."

"No!"

"So good to eat!"

"No!"

"Oh, take a little bite."

"No!"

"Come on, take a little bite."

"No!"

"Take a little bite."

"No!"

"God *won't* mind."

Adam and Eve paused, "Well . . . , maybe."

And it wasn't long before that "maybe" became an "Oh, one little bite won't matter."

Adam and Eve went up to the tree
Snatched that apple and took a bite!

The Garden of Eden went silent. The birds stopped singing. The bunnies stopped in their tracks. The wind stopped blowing, and Adam and Eve dropped the bitten apple. "Let's hide!" they cried and ran behind the tree. They looked at each other. "We can't hide from God," they said and came out from behind the tree.

"We made a mistake," they said.

"I know," said God.

"We took a bite,"

"I know," said God.

"We did what you said not to do."

"I know," said God.

"We have to leave the garden, don't we?"

"Yes, you do, and life will not be so easy. You will have to work hard and work together."

Adam and Eve began walking slowly and sadly away towards the edge of the garden. "Good-bye, God," they said. God replied, "Why do you say 'good-bye'?" They answered, "Because we won't see you again. You live in the garden and we are leaving, so we are sad—sad for making the mistake, and sad because we won't see you again."

God smiled, "Oh Adam and Eve, I will still be with you. I will *always* be with you and I will *always* love you. My love is everywhere. And from now on, people will make mistakes, and they will learn from these mistakes. Then they will understand how to move on. So go, but know that I will be with you. And because you have known the Garden, you can work to make the world a place where no one is cold or hungry and as peaceful and full of love as Eden."

And so Adam and Eve left the Garden of Eden and began their work together making the world a good place to live in, knowing that God's love was still with them.

Possible alternative ending

And that is what we have been doing ever since: working together, trying to make the world a more peaceful place where no one is cold or hungry.

AFTER THE STORY

And here at school, we all make mistakes too. That's part of being alive! And we're learning how to work together to make our world a more peaceful, beautiful place. Now let's all sing "In My Garden."

STORY-TELLING TIPS

- Note how Adam and Eve always say, "…we do not want to leave the garden," so the children know that Adam and Eve are very aware of the consequences if they taste the apple.
- You might want to have someone be the voice of the snake, or if you like being the snake, let someone or two be Adam and Eve saying, "No!"
- You can let the children say the "No!" for Adam and Eve. To do this, right in the middle of the story, say to the children, "Now I want you to be Adam and Eve saying, 'No.'" Then you tempt them with as many tantalizing taste-tingling things you can think of. They will love joining in. To move it to the next stage, then you change the pace—after they have said "No!" you say, "But then the snake said 'God won't mind' and Adam and Eve said, 'Maybe.'" Then you continue. They will feel good about having said the "No's" and even sadder for Adam and Eve.

ART NEEDS

- Adam and Eve
- Tree
- Big red apple
- Snake
- More of the garden with flowers, bushes, little animals (optional)

STORY SKELETON

- Adam and Eve are in garden.
- God tells them they will never be cold or hungry.
- Adam and Eve see apple and want to taste it.
- God says, "No, you cannot taste."
- They ask, "What if we do?"
- God says they will leave garden

- Adam and Eve enjoy the garden.
- They always wind up in front of tree.
- One day a snake is in the tree and calls to Adam and Eve.
- Snake asks them to try the apple.

Would You Like to Take a Bite?

(The Garden of Eden)

Bill Gordh

- Adam and Eve say, "No!"
- Snake asks again.

♫

- "No!"
- Snake keeps trying.

♫

- They say, "No!"
- Snake says, "God won't mind."
- They say, "OK."
- They bite apple.
- Adam and Eve hide.
- They realize they can't hide from God.
- God knows what has happened.
- They know God knows.
- They know they have to leave, but hope maybe they don't have to go.
- They have to go.
- They say "good-bye" to God.
- God says he will always be with them.
- They must go and work hard to try and make the world outside like the Garden of Eden, a place of peace where no one will be cold or hungry.

chapter 4

NOAH AND THE ARK

GENESIS 6 – 9:17

A Story about Faith and Working Together

Sing-along "Arkie, Arkie"

Images of Noah's ark full of animals are everywhere and familiar to many children who might not know the story. For those who do, the story continues to be a favorite. This telling does not focus on God's anger at people not working together and causing the flood. Rather, it begins like the old Bible song "Arkie, Arkie" with God coming to Noah and telling him there will be a flood. The story then describes Noah's faith in the word of God, and how Noah, his family, and the animals managed to make it successfully through the flood.

BEFORE THE STORY

The story today is from the Bible. It's about a man named Noah! The artwork is by _________ .

THE STORY

Long, long ago, God came to Noah. God said, "Noah,

It's gonna rain.

It's gonna rain, rain, rain, rain, rain.

Noah said to God, "But this is the desert. It never rains out here!"

God said it again, "Noah,

It's gonna rain.

It's gonna rain, rain, rain, rain, rain.

Noah said, "God, that sounds like you mean a lot of rain. How much?"

God answered, "Noah,

It's gonna rain.
It's gonna rain, rain, rain, rain, rain
for forty days and forty nights."

"What?" said Noah and God said it again, "Noah,

It's gonna rain.
It's gonna rain, rain, rain, rain, rain
for forty days and forty nights."

Noah said, "If it rains that much there will be a flood!"

"That's right," said God.

"If there's a flood, I'd better build a boat!"

"That's right," said God.

So Noah and his family got out their hammers and saws and started building a boat.

Tap, tap, tap, saw, saw, saw all day long.

The neighbors laughed, "This is the desert, Noah!"

Noah answered, "But God said, 'Noah,

It's gonna rain.
It's gonna rain, rain, rain, rain, rain
for forty days and forty nights.'

And that's why I'm building this boat." The neighbors laughed and walked away.

As soon as the boat was built, they stepped back and took a look. It was so big and beautiful, they gave it a name: "The Ark." But they did not have long to enjoy their work for over the hills came the animals. And how did they come?

They came two by two.

Here come the zebras, and how did they come?

They came two by two.

Here come the lions, and how did they come?

They came two by two.

Here come the elephants, and how did they come?

They came two by two.

Here come the dogs, and how did they come?

They came two by two.

Here come the cats and the bats and the monkeys and the llamas, and how did they come?

They came two by two.

And every animal that lives on this earth today came, and how did they come?

They came two by two.

When the last animal got on board, Noah closed the door.

The rain began—pitter-patter, pitter-patter and grew faster and faster and faster. It rained and rained and rained. The ark floated up on top of the water. The water grew deeper and deeper and deeper. It rained and rained and rained.

It rained for forty days and forty nights. The rain stopped. Noah opened the window and the trap door on the deck. They could see the blue, blue sky and the big beautiful sun.

"Can we get out?" asked the animals. "Not until there is land, " said Noah. He sent out a dove to look for a leaf. A leaf would mean the water was going down. The bird came back shaking its head. The next day, Dove flew off again. No leaf. The third day, Dove flew out again. . . . A leaf! She came back with a leaf.

The water went lower and lower and lower until the boat CLUNKED down on the ground. Noah opened the door and all the animals rushed outside. "Thank you, God, we're all OK!" said Noah. And that's what they did. They thanked God. And God came to Noah and said, "I am proud of you for taking care of all these animals, and everyone on the ark working together. There will never be another flood like this."

Then God made a curved shape of many colors—the first rainbow! and put it in the sky. "Let this rainbow remind you of peace, and that all creatures should take care of each other on this earth." Noah and his family and all the animals looked up at the rainbow and they smiled!

AFTER THE STORY

And that's the story of Noah, a person who never lost faith. And here at school we work and play together when it rains, and when the sun comes back again. Now let's sing "Arkie, Arkie."

STORY-TELLING TIPS

- The repetition of "rain" and other words in the story is to suggest rhythms that will propel the telling. If you find these a hindrance, you can simplify. For example, you can have God say to Noah, "It's going to rain (and rain and rain). It's going to rain for forty days and forty nights."
- When the animals are introduced, the text suggests specific animals, but it is more significant that you use the animals that the children decide to create. As long as they are in pairs, it is more fun for everyone that the animals are the ones suggested and created by the children.

ART NEEDS

- Noah
- Ark
- Pairs of animals
- Dove
- Waves (optional)
- Thunder clouds and lightning (optional)
- Rainbow

STORY SKELETON

- Noah lives in the desert.
- God tells Noah that rain is coming.
- It's going to rain for forty days and nights.
- Noah realizes that there will be a flood.
- Noah and his family begin building a big boat.
- Neighbors laugh at Noah building a boat.
- Noah believes God and keeps building.
- The boat is finished and named "The Ark."
- The animals come two by two.
- The rain comes.
- The waters rise.
- Forty days and nights of rain.
- Noah sends a dove out to find a leaf.
- Two days—no leaf.
- Day three—leaf!
- Thump! The ark hits the ground.
- Noah, family, and animals come out.
- They sing and dance.
- God puts a rainbow in the sky.
- The rainbow celebrates the animals and Noah working together and living in peace on the ark.
- The rainbow is also a promise that there will never be such a big flood again.

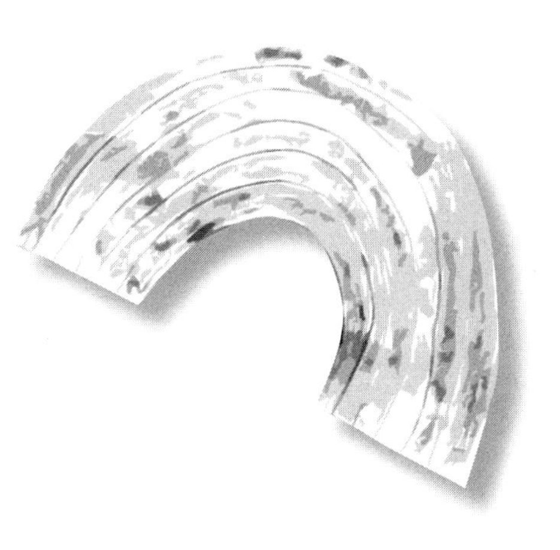

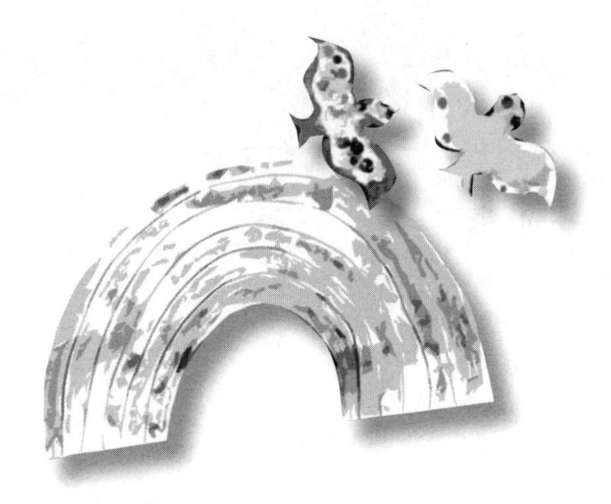

chapter 5

JONAH AND THE WHALE

JONAH 1:1 – 2:10

A Story about Doing What You Know You Should Do

Sing-along "Who Did Swallow Jonah?"

The telling of Jonah and the whale here is based on the notion than children know in their hearts what they should do. Of course, that does not mean they want to do what is called for. Thus in this story the use of the refrain

I don't want to go to Ninevah.
I don't want to go to Ninevah.
I don't want to go to Ninevah.
And I'm *not* gonna go.

We have all heard children boldly make this kind of statement and in fact felt this way ourselves. The story follows the consequences of this decision.

BEFORE THE STORY

Our story today is another story from the Bible. It is about a man named Jonah. The artwork is by ________ .

THE STORY

Jonah was a good man. He was a hard worker and a good neighbor. He was always ready to help. So when God came to Jonah to ask him a favor, you would think Jonah would have said, "Of course!" All God wanted was for Jonah to go over to the town of Ninevah. God said, "Jonah, I want you to go over to Ninevah and talk to those people. Talk to them about taking care of each other and working together. You are so good at those important things, and they can learn from you." For some reason, Jonah did not want to go, and he said to God,

♫ **I don't want to go to Ninevah.**
I don't want to go to Ninevah.
I don't want to go to Ninevah.
And I'm not gonna go.
No, I'm not gonna go.

God was surprised and told Jonah, "OK, Jonah. I'll leave you tonight to think about it, and we can talk again in the morning." Well that night Jonah went to bed. He couldn't sleep. He just lay there, staring at the ceiling and singing,

♫ **I don't want to go to Ninevah.**
I don't want to go to Ninevah.
I don't want to go to Ninevah.
And I'm not gonna go.
No, I'm not gonna go.

Toward the end of the night before dawn, Jonah got an idea. He decided he would sneak out of his house so when God came back to talk to him, he'd be gone. So Jonah got up, had his breakfast in the dark, sneaked out the back door, and went in the opposite direction from Ninevah, and as he walked he sang,

♫ **I don't want to go to Ninevah.**
I don't want to go to Ninevah.
I don't want to go to Ninevah.
And I'm not gonna go.
No, I'm not gonna go.

Jonah walked and walked and walked until he came to the sea. There he saw some people loading a fishing boat. He thought, "That's perfect. I've never been on a boat before, so God will never even think to look for me there." But does God know where Jonah is? Of course, he knows.

Anyway, Jonah got on the boat and the fishing did not go well. They did not catch one fish, and then the thunder started. The big dark clouds came rolling across the sky, and it started to rain, and the waves got bigger and bigger and bigger, and the ship rocked and rolled in that stormy sea. And suddenly Jonah was flying off that fishing boat and SPLASH! into the water. But even underwater Jonah was singing,

♫ **I don't want to go to Ninevah.**
I don't want to go to Ninevah.
I don't want to go to Ninevah.
And I'm not gonna go.
No, I'm not gonna go.

There's Jonah sinking in the water and then! A whale swam up and swallowed Jonah whole. Now we find Jonah in the great big smelly belly of the whale and Jonah says, "Uh-oh. I think I've made a big mistake." Jonah knelt down and prayed. He prayed and prayed and prayed, and when he said, "Amen," the whale began swimming up and up and up to the surface, and that great big whale let out a great big burp (You could hear it for 173 miles!), and Jonah went flying through the air. Luckily he landed on the shore. He dusted himself off and said, "I still want to sing, but I have some new words for my song. And he sang,

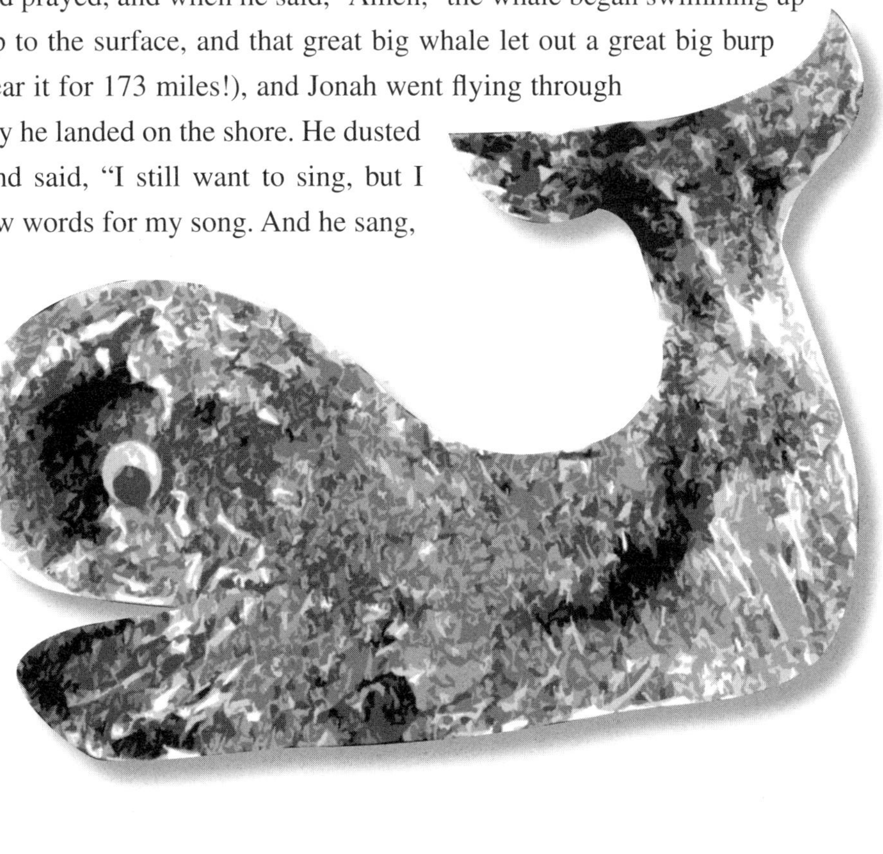

♫ **I sure want to go to Ninevah.**
I sure want to go to Ninevah.
I sure want to go to Ninevah.
And I'm going there today.
Yes, I'm going there today.

And he did! He went to Ninevah.

AFTER THE STORY

And just like Jonah, there are times all of us have things we don't want to do, things that we know we should do. Well this story is saying, "Just go ahead and do them."

And now we'll sing. "Who Did Swallow Jonah?"

STORY-TELLING TIPS

- When Jonah goes into the water and still sings his song, sing like you are underwater. It is very funny, and the children will laugh alleviating any fear created by the whale swallowing Jonah.
- If you decide not to sing the refrain, just use the simpler declaration, "I don't want to go to Ninevah, and I'm not going to go!"
- This telling does not have the fishing people throwing Jonah in the sea. It leaves his ocean entrance ambiguous as the focus is on Jonah ending up in the water.

ART NEEDS

- Jonah
- Fishing boat
- Whale
- Jonah's house (optional)

STORY SKELETON

- Jonah is a good friend and neighbor.
- God wants Jonah to go to Ninevah and show them how to be good neighbors.
- Jonah does not want to go and says

I Don't Wanna Go to Nineveh

(The Story of Jonah)

Bill Gordh

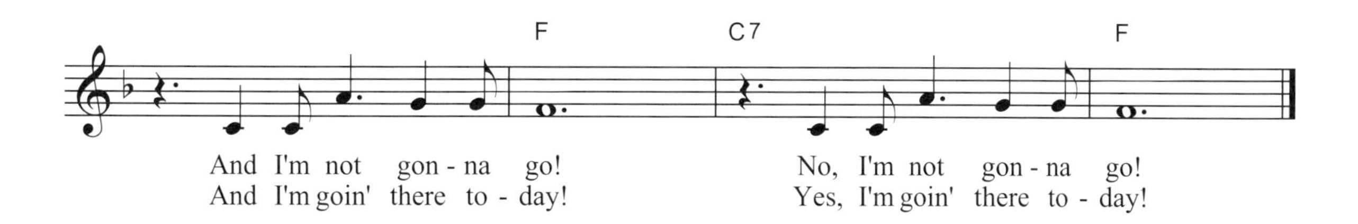

- God says he'll ask again tomorrow.
- Jonah goes home, eats dinner, and gets into bed.

♫

- Jonah decides to run away the next day.
- Jonah walks in the opposite direction from Ninevah singing his song.

♫

- Jonah comes to the sea.
- Jonah goes on the fishing boat, thinking God won't know where he is.
- Jonah flies off the boat, still singing his song.

♫

- Jonah is swallowed by a whale.
- In the bottom of the sea in the belly of the whale, Jonah prays.
- The whale swims up to the surface and burps out Jonah.
- Jonah lands on the shore and decides to go to Ninevah.

♫

chapter 6

JESUS AND THE THREE FISHERMEN
LUKE 5:1-11

A Story about Persistence and Trying New Ideas

Sing-along "Keep On Trying" (p. 247)

The telling of this story weaves an old Bible song into the narrative. The listeners sing the song when called for by the narrative, so everyone participates in the telling of the tale. This solidifies the group as they experience working together to tell the story. The story is often told to set up the idea of the "Fishers of Men," a quite complex thought. This telling focuses on the importance of persistence and trying ideas suggested by others.

BEFORE THE STORY

Our story today is once again from the Bible. It is about three fishermen—Peter and John and James, and what happened to them one day. The artwork is by ______.

THE STORY

Our story today is about three fishermen, Peter and John and James, and every day they took out their boat, loaded their nets, and sailed out into the sea.

♫ **Peter and John and James in a sailboat.**
Peter and John and James in a sailboat.
Peter and John and James in a sailboat
out on the beautiful sea.

They fished every day. That was their job. They caught fish to feed the people in their village. Usually they caught lots of fish, but on the day of this story, they were not having any luck.

They took out their boat like always.
Then they threw in the net.
They waited a little bit.
They pulled out the net.
Tell me, what did they get?
Nothing!
Not one fish! So they tried again,
They threw in the net.
They waited a little bit.
They pulled out the net.
Tell me what did they get?
Nothing!
Not one fish!
They tried again and again, but every time
They threw in the net.
They waited a little bit.
They pulled out the net.
Tell me what did they get?
Nothing!
Not one fish!

♫ **Well, they fished all day, but they caught nothin'.**
They fished all day, but they caught nothin'.
They fished all day, but they caught nothin'
out on the beautiful sea.

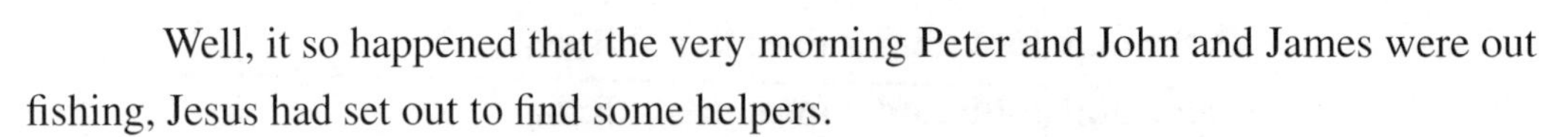

Well, it so happened that the very morning Peter and John and James were out fishing, Jesus had set out to find some helpers.

♫ **And Jesus came along walking by the water.**
Jesus came along walking by the water.
Jesus came along walking by the water
out on the beautiful sea.

He stopped and watched them. Peter and John and James decided to give up, but Jesus called out to them,

♫ **Why don't you throw your nets on the other side.**
Throw your nets on the other side.
Throw your nets on the other side
out on the beautiful sea.

Well, it was hard to hear his words across the water, and Peter and John and James really were fed up with fishing. Still they decided to ask the man what he said. They called out to Jesus, "What did you say?"

And Jesus sang again,

♫ **Why don't you throw your nets on the other side.**
Throw your nets on the other side.
Throw your nets on the other side
out on the beautiful sea.

Well, Peter and John and James realized they had only been fishing on one side of the boat, so they gave it a try.

And you know what?

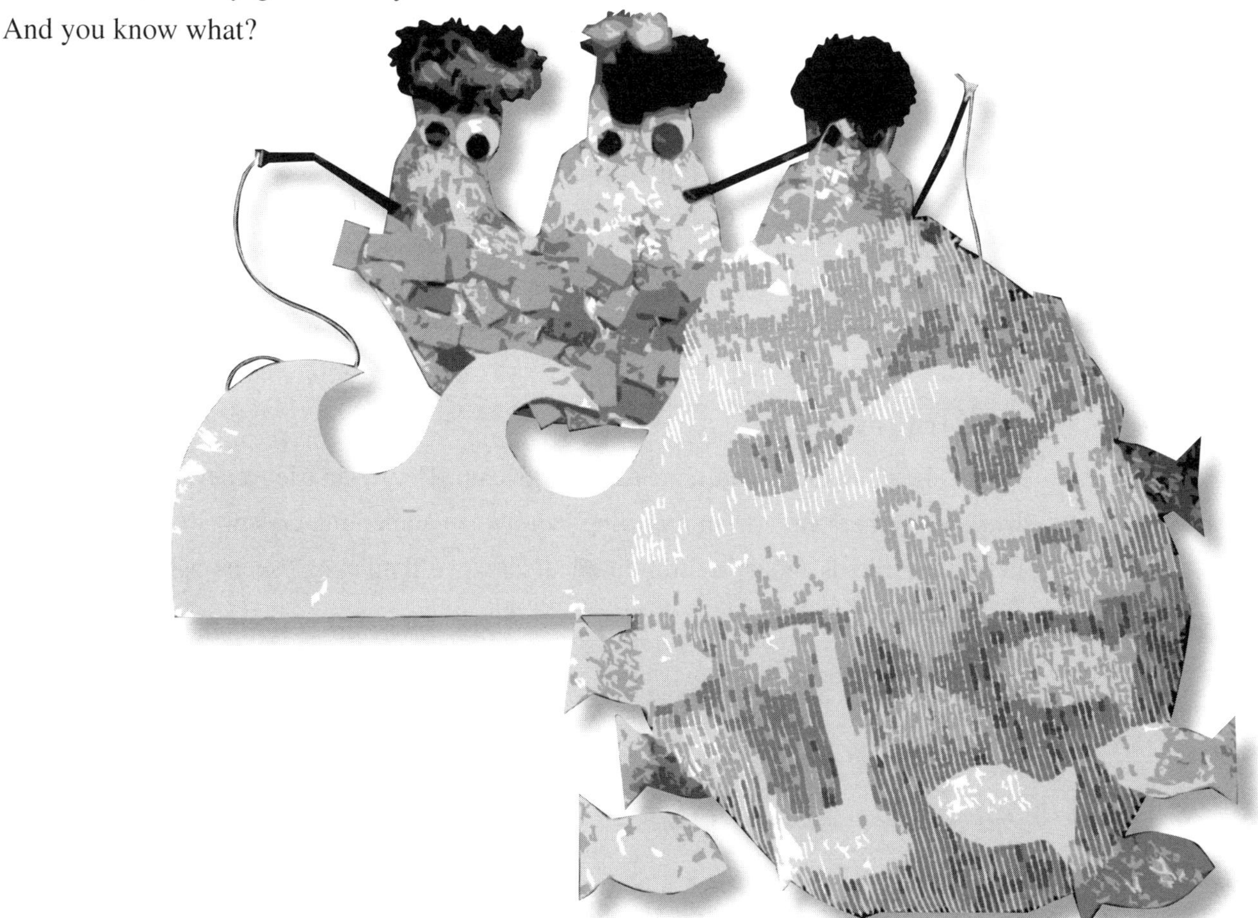

♫ **Now the nets were filled with great big fishes.**
The nets were filled with great big fishes.
The nets were filled with great big fishes
out on the beautiful sea.

Peter and John and James were sure glad they gave it another try with a new idea.

♫ **So the moral of the story is: Keep on trying.**
The moral of the story is: Keep on trying.
The moral of the story is: Keep on trying
wherever you may be!

So Peter and John and James sailed their boat back to shore and showed Jesus all the fish they had just caught and asked Jesus what he was doing. Jesus answered, "I am traveling from village to village telling everyone I see about the love of God and about sharing and caring and working together. Right now I'm trying to find some helpers." Peter and John and James asked Jesus if they could travel with him. "Yes, that would be great, "said Jesus, "but first let's take all the fish into the village. There are a lot of hungry people that would love some fresh fish."

So that's the story, and it all started with

♫ **Peter and John and James in a sailboat.**
Peter and John and James in a sailboat.
Peter and John and James in a sailboat
out on the beautiful sea.

AFTER THE STORY

Peter and John and James did not give up. They even tried a new idea, and that's what we do here. We "keep on trying" and when something doesn't work, we ask for help from friends and try a different idea. Now we'll all sing "Keep on Trying."

STORY-TELLING TIPS

- When you begin the story, name each of the fishermen and point to them (the children's artwork) on the boat, or place each in the boat as you name them. Say the names in the same order as the song.
- The throw-in-the-net verse is not part of the traditional song and is chanted rhythmically. After the first time they hear it, the children listeners will call out, "Nothing!"

ART NEEDS

- Jesus
- Three people fishing in a boat (Peter and John and James)
- Lots of fish
- A fishing net
- The sea (optional)

STORY SKELETON

- Peter and John and James in a sailboat.

♫

- They fish all day but they catch nothing.

♫

- Jesus came along.

♫

- Jesus said they should throw their nets on the other side of the boat.

♫ (two verses)

- They try his idea.
- They catch lots of fish.

♫

- Peter and John and James come to shore.
- Jesus tells them about his big job.
- They want to join him.
- First they take the fish to the village for people to eat.

♫

Peter and John and James

(Jesus and the Fishermen)

Traditional

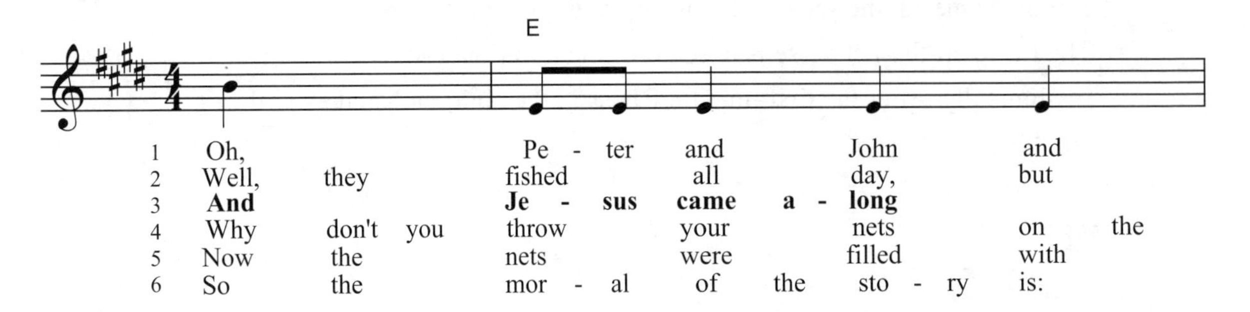

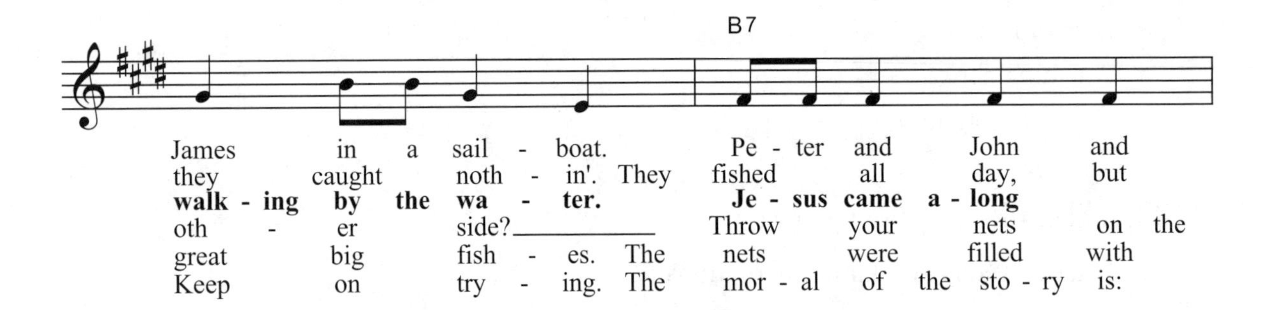

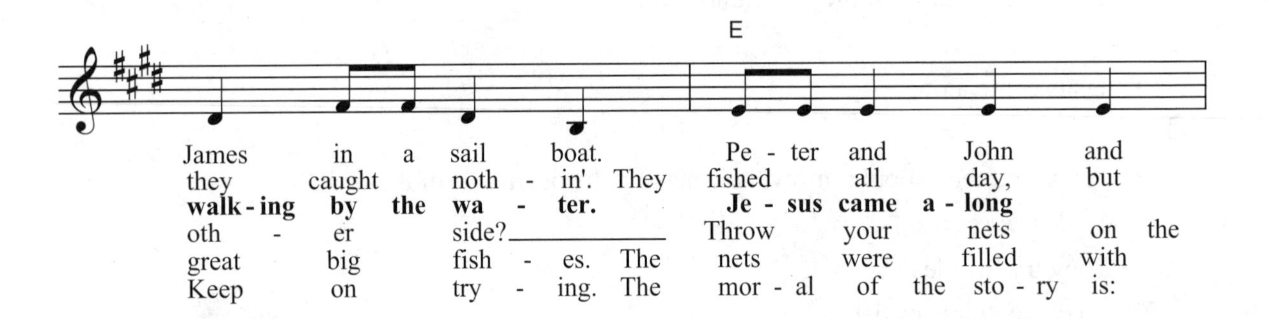

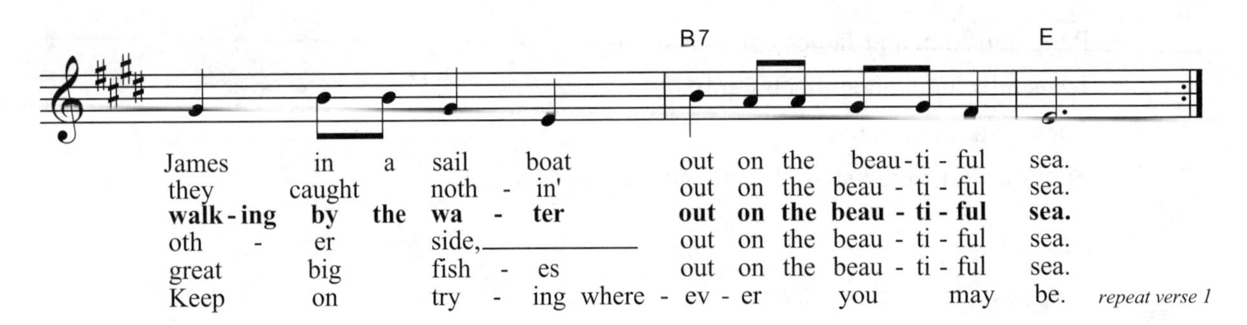

Verse 3 is bold to be a visual aid.

chapter 7

JESUS HEALS THE SICK
LUKE 17:11-19

A Story about Saying Thanks

Sing-along "I Want to Thank You" (p. 238)

The story of Jesus meeting and healing the lepers is a powerful tale of Jesus' acceptance of and love for all humankind. However, the focus here is on the person who returned to say, "Thank you." Children (and adults too for that matter) can forget to acknowledge generosity and this story provides an important reminder.

Some parents whose children have conditions that have no cures might feel uncomfortable with this story and the story of "The Lame Man Walks" (Chapter 15). You should discuss the story with these parents before including it in your gathering.

BEFORE THE STORY

Today's story is about Jesus and his love and care of everyone. The artwork is by ________ .

THE STORY

These were the days Jesus traveled from village to village with his stories of sharing and caring and love for each other and of God's love for everyone. Everywhere Jesus went there were crowds to greet him. One day as Jesus and his disciples walked toward a village a group of ten people waited along the side of the road. They were covered in bandages and clearly were sick. They moved closer and wanted to touch the man they had heard so much about. The disciples saw the sick people.

"Be careful Jesus!" cried the disciples. "They are lepers! Don't touch them. They will make you sick." These sad people had leprosy, a skin disease that causes terrible sores. People believed that leprosy was very easy to pass onto someone else, so people with the disease were made to live far from the villages, away from their families and friends. It turns out that leprosy is very hard to pass on, and most people cannot catch it at all, but back then people thought it was very contagious. Jesus looked at the sadness and hope in the eyes of the ten sick people.

The disciples spoke again, "Jesus, in the next village there is a large crowd waiting to see and hear you. Stay away from those lepers. We should move on." Jesus was still looking at the ten. Jesus smiled and thanked his helpers for their concern. "God loves everyone, my friends," he said. "God loves everyone." Then he moved closer to the bandaged, sad-hopeful people.

Jesus removed the bandages from one sick person after another. He moved his open hand across the sores on their legs and arms and bodies. He held each person close. One after another looked into his eyes and saw the love of God. Then each looked at his own arms or her own legs, and stomach and hands and elbows and feet and ankles and wrists and fingers and toes. The sores were gone! Their skin was clear and clean like a newborn baby. They were healed!

A man shouted with joy. A healed woman began to weep happy, joyous tears. One and another and another and another shouted and jumped and yelped and spun around and hugged each other and then raced for home. They ran because they needed to see those loved ones they missed so much. Jesus watched the people he had healed hurry off. Down the road and up over the hill and out of sight they ran, one after another.

But the last one, a little girl stopped at the top of the hill. Jesus watched her. Slowly she turned around and then, came running back down the hill. She ran up to Jesus all out of breath and full of the joy that comes from feeling good again after feeling terrible for so long. Jesus waited as the girl caught her breath. Then she said, "Jesus, I almost forgot. Thank you, thank you, thank you!" She hugged Jesus.

Then she turned and ran down the road, up over the hill and out of sight. This time she didn't stop until she was back home. There she leapt into the arms of her mother and father who could barely believe the miracle that had brought their daughter home. But she believed. She believed when she looked at her clear clean skin and she believed when she thought of the look in Jesus' eyes when she remembered to say, "Thanks, thanks a lot."

AFTER THE STORY

Here at school we sometimes forget to say, "Thanks." And that is why we tell this story as a reminder to notice and thank those who help us. Our sing-along is "I Want to Thank You."

STORY-TELLING TIPS

- It can be unsettling for some children to hear about leprosy, so consider your listeners before telling this story.
- Keep it simple and in your own words. The love and care comes out in the simplicity of the telling; thus no rhymes.

ART NEEDS

- Jesus
- A few disciples
- Sick people with bandages that can be removed
- The girl who comes back

STORY SKELETON

- Jesus travels on with his disciples.
- Ten people with leprosy wait along the road to see Jesus.
- The disciples warn Jesus to stay away.
- Jesus goes to the people anyway.
- He takes off their bandages.
- He passes his hand over their sores.
- Jesus hugs them.
- They look in the eyes of Jesus and see the love of God.
- They are healed.
- They are happy.
- They jump for joy.
- They run for home.
- A girl heads for home but then stops.
- She comes back to say, "Thanks."

chapter 8

THE GOOD SAMARITAN
LUKE 10:30-37

A Story about Helping Others

Sing-along "You've Got Me" (p. 258)

When we as grown-ups find ourselves steering young children away from the homeless or others on the street, it is important to continue remembering and telling the story of the Good Samaritan. There's a story of a child asking a grown-up why he didn't give some money to a person on the street who clearly needed it. The reply to the child was, "We can't give money to everyone who asks for it." The child's wise response was, "It was only one person."

The way the story is told here encourages children to be Good Samaritans in everyday life within their safe community. After all, they often forget to help each other, and this story reminds everyone of the importance of a helping hand.

BEFORE THE STORY

Today we are sharing another story from the Bible, a story that Jesus told about a man who needed some help. The artwork is by ___________ .

THE STORY

Jesus and his disciples continued their travels. Everywhere they went, Jesus spoke of the love of God, about sharing and caring and working together. He also talked about the importance of being a good neighbor and treating each other kindly. One day, someone in the crowd asked, "Jesus, what is a good neighbor?" and Jesus told the story of The Good Samaritan:

There was once a man traveling down the road from Jerusalem to Jericho. It was early in the morning and the road was empty. Suddenly two robbers jumped from behind a bush and attacked the man. They stole his money and knocked him to the ground. They kicked and beat him. Then they rolled him off the side of the road down into a ditch where he would not be seen. Then the robbers ran off.

The hurt man was scared and badly injured. He cried out,

♫ **O-O-O-OH, won't you lend me a hand?**
O-O-O-OH, someone, won't you lend me a hand?

But the road was empty. After a while the hurt man heard footsteps. Someone was coming up the road. He sang out,

♫ **O-O-O-OH, won't you lend me a hand?**
O-O-O-OH, someone, won't you lend me a hand?

The traveler heard the cry, but did not stop. In fact she crossed to the other side of the road and walked by as quickly as possible. The hurt man was still alone, lying in the ditch, hoping for some help. He heard some more footsteps. He sang out,

♫ **O-O-O-OH, won't you lend me a hand?**
O-O-O-OH, someone, won't you lend me a hand?

The next traveler was a merchant who bought and sold goods, and he was on his way to Jericho. He heard the cry of the hurt man, but he had business in Jericho and no time to stop. The merchant passed by without a word.

The road was empty again. The hurt man sang out,

♫ **O-O-O-OH, won't you lend me a hand?**
O-O-O-OH, someone, won't you lend me a hand?

He heard footsteps and before he could sing out again, he heard a voice asking, "Are you all right?" The hurt man looked up at the stranger. The man was from Samaria on his way to Jericho, and he had heard the hurt man's cry. The man told the Good Samaritan what had happened. The Samaritan helped the hurt man out of the ditch, but the injured man's leg was broken. "Put your arm over my shoulder," the Good Samaritan said, "I'll help you walk."

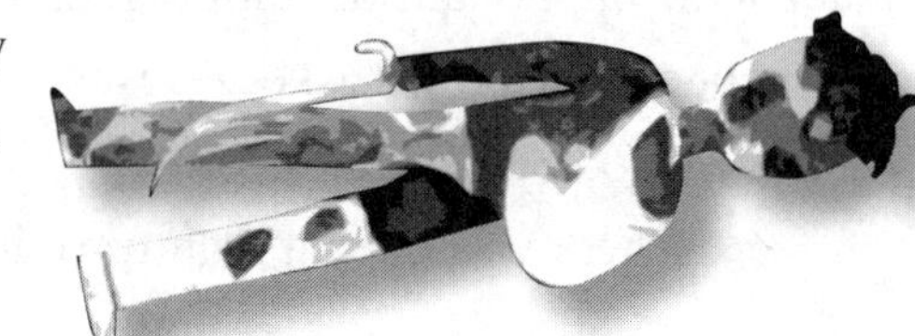

They walked together until they came to an inn. The innkeeper came out to help. The Good Samaritan asked, "Can my friend stay here?" and the innkeeper nodded his head. "There is always room in my inn," said the innkeeper. The hurt man spoke, "But I have no money. It was stolen!" The Good Samaritan reached into his own pocket and paid the innkeeper, and before he left the Samaritan said, "I'll be back tomorrow to see how you are feeling."

As the Good Samaritan walked away, the hurt man and the innkeeper watched him. The innkeeper said to the hurt man, "You have a really good friend there." The hurt man nodded and smiled. "I never met him before."

The story was over and Jesus looked at the crowd, "Now who was the good neighbor?" Everyone said, "The Good Samaritan." Jesus smiled and nodded. But then a boy asked, "But Jesus, we always travel together, and we have never seen a robber. So why did you tell that story?" And Jesus answered, "You may always travel with others and you may never see a robber, but you will see someone fall or a friend who needs some help. When you do you can choose to keep on walking, or you can be a Good Samaritan and help your neighbor.

AFTER THE STORY

And here at school, we all try to be good Samaritans and help our friends when they get hurt. We will sing "You've Got Me!"

STORY-TELLING TIPS

- At the beginning, after telling of Jesus' travel, PAUSE before starting the story of the Good Samaritan. A story within a story is a little tricky and the separation should be made. You can also use the art to assist you, by introducing it once you begin the Samaritan parable.

- At the end of the story, when you describe Jesus asking the crowd about who is the good neighbor, you can address the question to the children so that they answer the question out loud and help you make your point. You might even say, "That's right and with your answer you just helped me finish telling the story. Thank you!"
- Note that the man from Samaria is repeatedly referred to as the "Good Samaritan" in the telling, as though "good" was part of his name. This helps the children make a stronger connection to this character and the theme of the story.

ART NEEDS

(We do not represent the robbers as it too easily plays into stereotypes.)

- Traveler/injured person
- Two separate travelers who pass on by
- The Good Samaritan
- The inn (optional)
- The innkeeper

STORY SKELETON

- Jesus continues travels, sharing stories.
- Jesus mentions being a good neighbor and someone asks what a good neighbor is.
- Jesus tells the story of "The Good Samaritan."
- A man is walking down the road from Jerusalem to Jericho.
- Robbers jump him and steal his money.
- They push him into a ditch.
- He calls for help.
- But there is no one.
- He hears someone coming.

Lend Me a Hand

(The Good Samaritan)

Bill Gordh

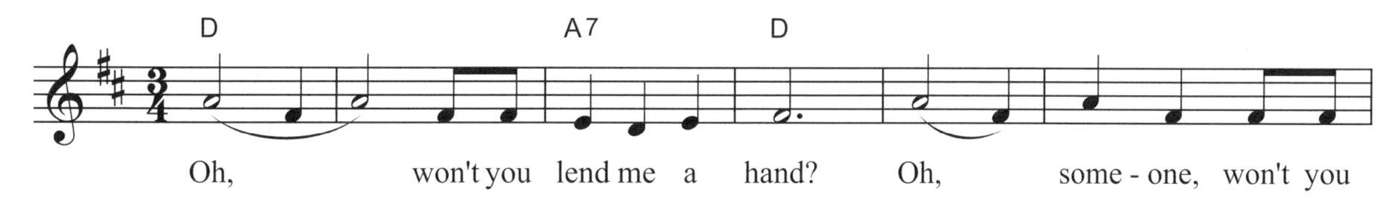

- The first passer by moves to the other side of the road and walks by quickly.
- The hurt man hears footsteps again and calls out.

♫

- The next traveler is a merchant who's in a hurry.
- The merchant goes on by.
- The hurt man hears footsteps and calls out again.

♫

- It is a man from Samaria—the Good Samaritan.
- The Good Samaritan stops.
- The Good Samaritan helps the hurt man walk to an inn.
- The Good Samaritan pays for the room and food.
- The Good Samaritan leaves.
- The innkeeper remarks on what a good friend the hurt man has.
- The hurt man says he never met the Samaritan before.
- The story is over and Jesus asks who was the good neighbor.
- Everyone says, "The Good Samaritan!"
- A child says that friends aren't on a road alone and they never saw a robber.
- Jesus says that it might be true, but there will be a time when a friend falls or needs some help.
- Then each person decides if she will walk on by or be a Good Samaritan.

part 3

STORIES OF FAMILY AND FRIENDS

chapter 9

THE NAMING OF THE ANIMALS
GENESIS 2:19-20

A Story about Friendship

Sing-along "You've Got Me" (p. 258)

Basing an entire chapel on two Bible verses may be a stretch, but young children always enjoy stories of animals. The notion of naming all the animals is an exciting one for them. Bob Dylan wrote a wonderful song called "Man Gave Names to All the Animals" in which each verse describes a creature, and the final rhyme is the name of that animal. I have taken that idea and brought it to a wide range of animals. These verses ask children to use the information given and their rhyming skills to correctly predict the name of the animal. The story then moves from the naming of animals to the name/description of a relationship—friendship. Although the Bible story suggests that Adam named the animals before Eve was created, we have the two naming them together to make it a more inclusive story for all the young listeners.

BEFORE THE STORY

Today's story is from the Bible and tells about Adam and Eve in the Garden of Eden. The artwork is by __________ .

THE STORY

Adam and Eve loved the Garden of Eden. It was such a beautiful place to run and dance and climb and jump and sing. Then they got a special job. God asked them to name all the animals! Every animal that walked on four legs or two or no legs at all would need to have its own name. They would have to find a word for each of the flapping creatures in the air and those swimming around in the water, the tree climbers, the hole-diggers, the hoppers, the leapers, the racers, and the slow pokes. Each and everyone deserved its own wonderful name. So they looked around.

And what did they see?
Well, it did have a bark.
But it wasn't a log.
A tree with four legs?
No, let's call it a ________. (DOG)

So Adam and Eve played fetch with the dog and ran with it across the open fields in the garden. Then they saw something long and slim moving across the ground. Now what to call this one?

On its belly it slithers.
Oh, its belly must ache!
Scaly, not scary.
Let's call it a _________. (SNAKE)

They watched the snake slither away, past the apple tree and into the tall grass. After that Adam and Eve named the elephant "Elephant" and the rhino "Rhinoceros" and the leopard they called "Leopard" and the ape they named "Ape."

They called the fast one a "Cheetah,"
And the slow one a "Snail,"
The climber a "Chimpanzee"
With its short little tail.

Then Adam and Eve decided to name some of the marvelous water creatures.

They named one a "Dolphin"
As it dove in the sea.
Then they named a "Jelly Fish"
And a "Sea Anemone."
They named a strange one a "Squid"
As it left an inky trail.

Then they saw a water spout

And named the big one a _________. (WHALE)

They looked up in the sky and there were wondrous winged creatures flying above them. They named the sparrows and the hawks, the blue jays and the chickadees. They named the eagle and the condor. They saw a bird walking toward them and it spread its beautiful tail feathers. They called it a peacock.

They named the duck and the turkey
The chick and rooster too.
They heard a quack, a peep, a gobble,
And a cock-a-doodle-do.

Then Adam and Eve started naming the bugs.
They named the doodle-bug and lady bug,
The fly, and the flea.
The centipede and beetle,
The butterfly and bee.

What a day it was! Naming all these magnificent creatures was a wonderful job. Adam and Eve were working together, talking it over, taking care of each other, and they looked around them at the beautiful garden. And then they looked at each other. "What's a name for what we are?" they wondered. They looked at each other some more, and they both said it at the same time, "Friends! We're friends." And that is the story of the naming of the animals and the first two friends.

AFTER THE STORY

And that's what we all are here at school—friends. We talk and listen and take care of each other. That's what friends have always done. And now we'll sing "You've Got Me".

STORY-TELLING TIPS

- You may want to put the animal rhymes on index cards and tell the story between cards. You could even shuffle them and surprise yourself. The cards could then be given to the classroom teachers to use with the children.
- Some older classes might want to create their own animal rhymes for this story. Guessing the rhymes is great fun for the children, and the younger ones will like the guessing game even more after they know the answers. The theme of friendship is an important one, so this chapel can easily be repeated. You might get ideas from the children about the qualities of friendship and incorporate them into the story. The more the children have to do with this story, the more fun for everyone.

ART NEEDS

- Adam
- Eve
- Dog
- Snake
- A sea creature
- A flying animal
- Any or all of the other animals named in the story or additional favorites from the classes

STORY SKELETON

- Adam and Eve in the garden enjoying themselves—singing and dancing and playing.
- God gives them a job to name the animals.
- They name the land animals.
- They name the flying animals.
- They name the water creatures.
- They need a name for each other.
- They call each other "friends."

chapter 10

ABRAHAM AND LOT
GENESIS 12:1 – 13:17

A Story about Sharing

Sing-along "Work a Little Bit" (p. 242)

Children appreciate hearing a story about grown-ups having a hard time with sharing. They also are reassured with the realization that this difficulty has been going on for such a long time. This makes the close of the story when the two friends talk and find a solution even more powerful. It also suggests that sometimes separating arguing friends, rather than trying to "work it out" then and there, gives each the space she or he needs.

BEFORE THE STORY

Today's story is from the Bible about a very wise man named Abraham. The artwork is by _______ .

THE STORY

Once there was a man named Abraham. He lived in a land called Ur with his wife Sarah. They were happy living in Ur with their family and friends. They had great flocks of sheep and many people working for them.

One day God spoke to Abraham. God said, "Abraham, I want you to move from this land. I have big plans for you."

"I don't mind moving," said Abraham, " if that's what you think I should do. But where?"

God said, "Abraham, don't worry about where. You'll know when you have arrived and you'll be happy. Where you're going, the land is beautiful and full of life."

Abraham told Sarah what God had said. Sarah looked at her husband and said, "Well, Abraham. It sounds like we should start packing." And that's what they did. As they were packing, Abraham's cousin Lot came by. He was curious.

"Abraham, why are you packing?" asked Lot.

"God told us of a new land where he wants us to live. He said it is beautiful and full of life. "

"That sounds great!" said Lot. "Could my family come too?"

Abraham and Sarah welcomed Lot to join them on their journey. They set out with their families and the people who worked with them as well as all their sheep. They traveled over hills. They traveled through valleys. They traveled across rivers. They traveled until they came to a land called Canaan.

When Abraham saw Canaan, he knew it was the place God had told him about. It was a beautiful land, and there just up the hill from a stream stood a huge oak. Abraham went and stood beneath the magnificent tree and looked up. There were more branches than he could count. The feeling that this great tree gave him made Abraham confident. "We'll be happy here, Sarah," said Abraham.

They were happy and so were the sheep, for there was plenty of green, green grass. The sheep were content and peaceful, and so were the shepherds—for a while.

Then the shepherds who worked for Abraham began to have arguments with the shepherds who worked for Lot. The first arguments were just about little things, but before long it seemed like they argued about everything. Often the disagreements were about who owned what.

"<u>Your</u> sheep are eating <u>my</u> grass!" shouted Abraham's shepherds.

"<u>Your</u> sheep are drinking <u>my</u> water," said one of Lot's shepherds.

"That's not <u>your</u> water!

"It's <u>my</u> water, " was the response.

"No, it's mine."

"It's mine!"

"It's mine!"

"Well, <u>your</u> sheep are eating <u>my</u> grass."

"That's not <u>your</u> grass, it's <u>mine</u>!"

Abraham was sitting beneath the great oak when he heard the fights going back and forth, back and forth.

"Mine."

"No, mine!"

"No, mine!"

Abraham listened to the shepherds argue. He walked to the top of the hill and looked across the beautiful new land. He could still hear the shepherds arguing. He thought about what was happening. They traveled all this way for something very special, and this land is very special, but now everyone is fighting.

"It's mine!"

"It's mine!"

"It's mine!"

Abraham got an idea. He called to Lot as he walked back down the hill. Lot came over and sat with Abraham beneath the oak. Abraham said, "Listen, Lot." Lot looked at Abraham and listened. He thought Abraham was going to say something. But then he realized Abraham wanted him to listen to the workers. Lot listened.

"It's mine!"

"It's mine!"

"It's mine!"

Lot looked at Abraham shaking his head and said, "What do we do?"

Abraham said, "Follow me." They went together to the top of the hill. Abraham pointed toward a nearby grassy hillside and said, "Why don't you and your shepherds take your sheep and settle there. My shepherds can stay here. It is all beautiful land and if we know whose land is whose, then maybe we can share." Lot thought about it. He nodded and smiled, "That's a great idea!"

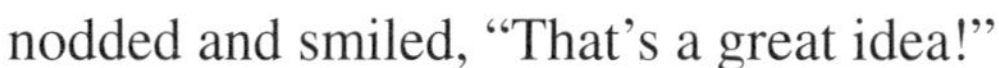

Lot and his shepherds moved their sheep to the new hillside and there was plenty of grass for all the sheep. After that, sometimes you'd hear one of Lot's shepherds saying to one of Abraham's shepherds, "My grass is green, green, green. Why don't you bring your sheep over here and let them graze for a while." Abraham watched as his shepherds led some sheep up Lot's hillside.

Abraham sat beneath the big oak and thought about sharing.

AFTER THE STORY

And like the story from so long ago, we all have trouble sharing sometimes, but if we talk and listen to each other we can figure out how to make it work. Now we'll all sing "Work a Little Bit."

STORY-TELLING TIPS

- You might have two grown-ups represent the arguing shepherds saying, "It's mine!" It adds a nice dynamic and makes it more real and more fun for the children listeners.
- You can use dialog when you tell the story like it is presented or if you are more comfortable you can keep the story in the third person, i.e., "When Abraham told his wife Sarah what God had told him, she suggested that they start packing." As you tell the stories more, you will become more comfortable including dialog that makes it more engaging for the children.

ART NEEDS

- Abraham
- Sarah
- Lot
- Some shepherds who work for Abraham
- Some shepherds who work for Lot
- Sheep of Abraham
- Sheep of Lot
- An oak tree

STORY SKELETON

- Abraham and Sarah live in the land of Ur.
- God tell Abraham he should move.
- God tells Abraham the new land will be beautiful.
- Abraham and Sarah agree to go.
- Lot, Abraham's cousin, wants to bring his sheep and shepherds too.
- Abraham and Sarah invite Lot to come along.
- They travel.
- They reach the land of Canaan.
- There is a huge oak tree where Abraham likes to sit.
- It is beautiful land.
- The shepherds of Abraham begin arguing with the shepherds of Lot.
- They argue about the water and the grass. "It's mine!" fills the air.
- Abraham listens to the arguing.
- Abraham and Lot talk.
- They decide to have two different places next to each other.
- Each can have a place where they can say, "It's mine."
- Each is more willing to share.

chapter 11

JOSEPH AND HIS FAMILY
GENESIS 37 – 44

A Story about the Importance of Family and Forgiveness

Sing-along "Love Begins with Giving" (p. 240-241)

The story of Joseph is a complex saga that could easily take many chapel sessions to include all the twists and turns in the plot. However for this volume, it is used as a single story to illustrate the importance of family and forgiveness. It also highlights Joseph learning to listen—an important part of growing up! The choices for inclusion or exclusion of details are based on its support of the theme while staying true to the "whole" story in spirit.

This telling is sympathetic to the hurt feelings of the brothers when Joseph receives the gift of the coat, and they are given nothing. The sequence of events that describe Joseph thrown into a pit by his brothers, the killing of a goat, spreading goat blood on his coat, and selling him to some travelers has been eliminated. A simple but powerful rejection by his brothers replaces this series of actions yet stays true to Joseph's emotional experience.

BEFORE THE STORY

Today's story is about a very big family and one of the younger brothers named Joseph who receives a very special present. The artwork is by ______ .

THE STORY

Once there was a boy named Joseph. Joseph was one of the younger children in a very big family: twelve children, as a matter of fact. Joseph liked doing lots of things, but what he loved most were his dreams. He enjoyed waking up in the morning, thinking about his dreams, and trying to figure out what they meant. He also loved talking about them. Every morning, after he got up, he followed his brothers around telling them his latest dream and what he thought it meant. Every morning, every day, day after day! For a while the brothers enjoyed hearing about Joseph's dreams, but they got tired of hearing the dreams every day, day after day. Then came the coat!

Joseph's father, Jacob loved all his children, but it seemed he loved Joseph more. This made the brothers sad and mad. One day, Jacob made a big mistake. He gave Joseph a beautiful coat, a coat of many colors, but he didn't give the other children anything. They watched as Joseph tried on his beautiful new coat.

Of course Joseph loved his coat, and he wore it proudly day and night. When Joseph asked, "Isn't this a beautiful coat?" the brothers had to agree because it was dazzling! It was a coat of many colors—like a rainbow! Who wouldn't want a coat like that? Joseph wore it all the time, and it reminded the brothers that their father had not given them something. So now when Joseph followed his brothers in his beautiful coat of many colors and talked about his dreams, it was too much. They turned on him and said, "Go away!" Joseph looked at them and asked, "What?" and they sang it out,

♫ **Go away, go away, go away, go away!**
We don't like your dreams anymore!

Joseph said, "But I want to tell you my dreams. They are important. OK, I won't talk about dreams today, but did you happen to notice how the gold in my coat gleams in the sunlight?"

This made the brothers even angrier and they said, "We don't like your coat. Just go away!" Joseph exclaimed, "What?" and they sang it out,

♫ **Go away, go away, go away, go away!**
We don't like your coat anymore!

They tore his coat off his back and threw it to the ground. Joseph said, "Give it back! I love my coat."

Now the brothers said, "Too bad. Just go away, Joseph." And they sang it out;

♫ **Go away, go away, go away, go away!**
We don't want you 'round anymore!

Joseph looked at his brothers, "But you're my family; you're my brothers."

But the brothers said, "We don't care."

♫ **Go away, go away, go away, go away!**
We don't want you 'round anymore!

So Joseph went away—sad, sad, sad. He traveled and traveled and traveled all the way to Egypt to the city of the king, the Pharaoh. There he grew. He found a house and worked in Egypt. During this time, Joseph still thought about dreams, and he began thinking about listening—listening to other people's dreams instead of just telling his own. The word spread about Joseph's ability to explain dreams, so when the Pharaoh had some strange dreams, he asked to see Joseph. Joseph had never met a pharaoh before and was very nervous, but the Pharaoh was kind and welcomed Joseph into his inner chambers. He told Joseph his dreams.

In my dream there were seven fat cows
Now Joseph tell me what could that mean?
In my dream there were seven skinny cows
Now Joseph tell me what could that mean?
And in my dream the seven skinny cows ate up the seven fat cows.
It was in my dream, in my dream,
So Joseph, tell me what could that mean?

Joseph thought about it, "Seven fat cows! Seven fat cows!" Joseph got an idea. He said, "Pharaoh, I think the seven fat cows mean that there will be seven years of plenty of food. Everything you plant in the whole kingdom will grow!"

"That's good," said the Pharaoh, "But what about the seven skinny cows eating up the seven fat cows?"

"Well," said Joseph. "The seven skinny cows eating the seven fat cows mean that after the seven great years, there will be seven terrible years of famine where nothing will grow."

"Ooh, "said the Pharaoh, "That's bad. What can we do?"

Joseph thought about it. He said, "Pharaoh, your dream gives us a chance to prepare. We can make a plan!"

"But what plan?" asked the Pharaoh.

Joseph thought some more. "Well, Pharaoh," said Joseph, "It seems to me, that during the seven years of plenty, we can eat what we need and save the rest. Then when the crops are not growing the following seven years, we will have the stored food for everyone."

"That's a great idea!" said the Pharaoh, "But how will we do it?"

"We can build great storage bins and store the extra food there. Then we can give food out to people when the crops stop growing. That way everyone will be safe"

The Pharaoh smiled, "Excellent thinking, Joseph. I am putting you in charge of carrying out this plan."

Sure enough, seven years of huge crops followed. There was so much food people could not believe it, but because of Joseph they were not foolish. They saved. They built great storage barns and stored food. After the seven years of glorious crops, the rains stopped and nothing grew at all. Nothing. But they had saved enough to feed everyone! Pharaoh sent out word that people could come and receive food from the storage bins Joseph had set up. People lined up for miles and had a long wait for food, but no one went hungry, for there was food for everyone.

Now, far from Egypt, there lived a large family who was very hungry. It was Joseph's family. They decided to make the long trip to stand in line and receive some food. They had not seen or heard of Joseph in these many years. When they got there they stood in line. As they moved closer they saw the man who was giving out the food. They couldn't believe it! It was their brother Joseph. Uh-oh! They got nervous. What would Joseph say to them? They had been so mean to him. They made him go away and now their brother was sharing food with the whole kingdom. They hoped he would not recognize them, and so they stooped their shoulders and looked down at the ground as they stepped closer.

Finally it was their turn. They held out their hands with their heads down, still staring at the ground. But Joseph knew who they were. He said, "Look at me!" The brothers looked up into Joseph's eyes. They did not find anger. They did not find hate. They found love, a brother's love.

"Aren't you angry, Joseph?" they asked, and Joseph said, "Not anymore,

♫ **Once a brother, always a brother.**
Once a sister always shall be.
Family is family and we are all family—
Brothers and sisters, you and me.

They hugged. They hugged and hugged and hugged.

♫ **Family is family and we are all family—**
Brothers and sisters, you and me.

AFTER THE STORY

And here at _________ "we are all family" ready to help each other. Let's sing "Love Begins with Giving."

STORY-TELLING TIPS

- You might illustrate Joseph following his brothers around telling them his dreams to present him as a bit of a pest. "Let me tell you my dream!" "Let me tell you my dream!" over and over again.
- When Joseph "goes away" the text says, "traveled and traveled and traveled." It is repeated three times to suggest the long trip in a simple way. Telling this part in a loping rhythm will further help separate the first part of the story from the new life in Egypt.
- You may want to keep the story with twelve brothers or twelve brothers and sisters.

ART NEEDS

- Joseph
- Twelve brothers/sisters
- Maybe Joseph's father (optional)
- Multicolored coat (that can be put on Joseph and taken off)
- Pharaoh

STORY SKELETON

- Joseph has twelve brothers (and sisters).
- Joseph tells his dreams to them all the time.
- Joseph receives a coat of many colors from his father, Jacob.
- Jacob does not give presents to the others.
- Brothers tell Joseph to go away.

Go Away!

(The Story of Joseph)

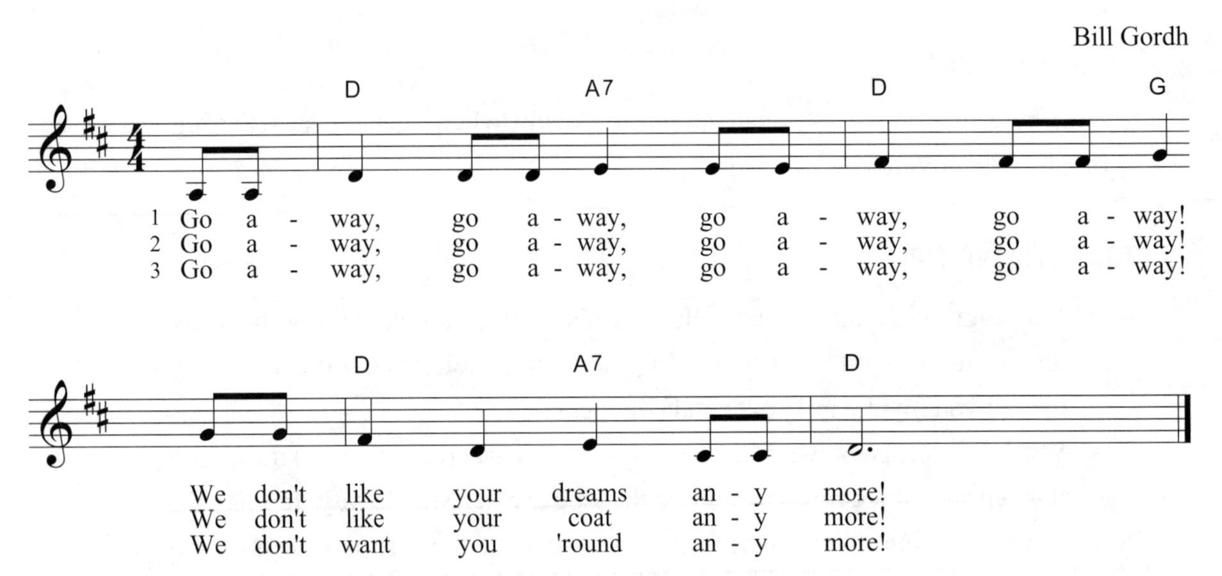

- Joseph persists.

♫

- Brothers take coat.

♫

- Joseph protests.

♫

- Joseph leaves and goes to Egypt.
- Joseph learns to listen and to interpret dreams.
- The pharaoh dreams of seven skinny cows eating seven fat cows.
- Joseph explains the dream: Seven years of plenty. Seven years of no food.
- Joseph suggests saving food during the seven good years.
- Joseph is put in charge of the food project.
- A barn is built and food is stored for the seven years of plenty.
- Seven years of drought follow.
- Joseph hands out food.
- Everyone comes.
- His brothers (and sisters) are hungry.
- They travel to Egypt.
- They see Joseph.
- They try and hide their faces so Joseph won't recognize them.
- Joseph recognizes brothers (and sisters).
- Joseph welcomes them.

Once a Brother, Always a Brother

(Story of Joseph)

Bill Gordh

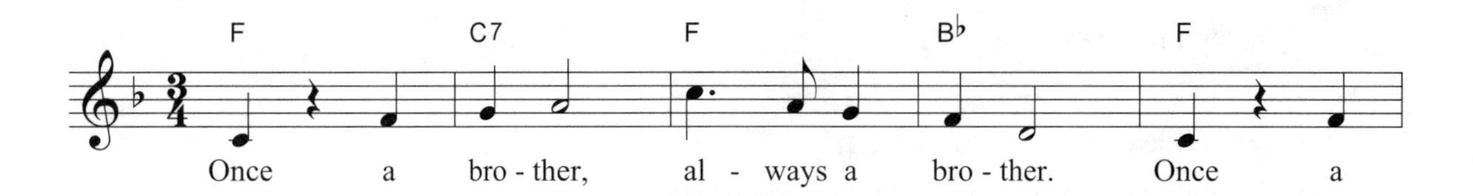

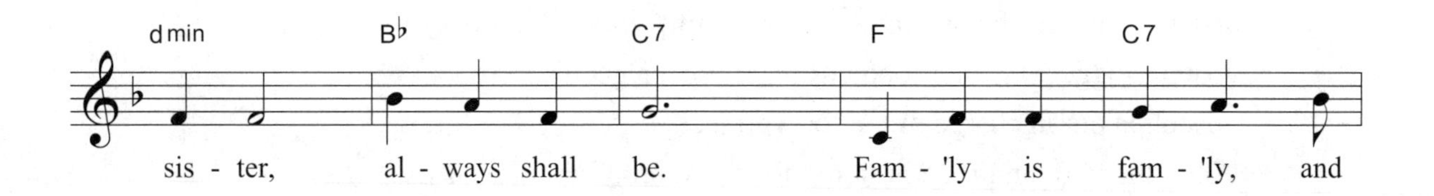

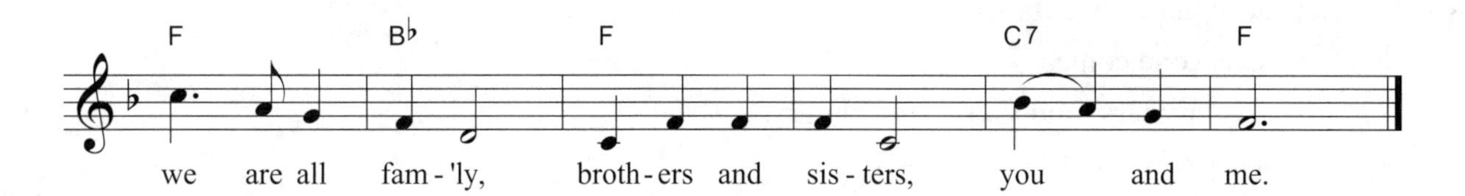

- They all hug.

♫ reprise of last two lines

chapter 12

RUTH AND NAOMI

RUTH 1:1 – 4:16

A Story about Friendship

Sing-along "You've Got Me" (p. 258)

Friendship is an important part of every school program. When our teachers speak to the class they often refer to the group as "friends." Hearing a beautiful story about looking out for someone else, especially an elderly person is reassuring to children. The complexity of the relationships described in the Bible has led to a telling that focuses on the friendship of Ruth and Naomi.

There are many more Bible stories with males as the central characters than females, so this story is especially valuable to share. You will notice that whenever possible, boys *and* girls are included in the stories. Further, when selecting non-Bible stories for chapel, you should consider finding stories with a female as the main character (See Part Seven).

BEFORE THE STORY

This Bible story is about friendship, a story about a woman named Ruth and her good friend Naomi. The artwork is by ________ .

THE STORY

This is a story of friendship. It's about a woman named Ruth and her great friend Naomi. Naomi was an old woman who lived alone in a small house on the edge of the village. Ruth was a young woman who also lived in the village. Ruth had many, many friends for she was kind, and she loved people. She had friends who were children and friends who were grown-ups, but her very best friend was Naomi. No matter how busy Ruth was, there was always time for Naomi. Always. Always.

Each and every evening Ruth stopped by Naomi's house to share supper. Together they would sit and eat and talk about the day. Often, very often, Naomi told Ruth about her younger days, when she, Naomi was a girl. She talked about growing up in the little town of Bethlehem. Ruth loved to hear these stories and think about what it was like for Naomi growing up in that land far away. Ruth looked at Naomi as she spoke. She saw how Naomi's face changed as she remembered those early times. Ruth watched tears fill Naomi's eyes as she talked. Naomi missed her childhood home.

One evening when Ruth came to Naomi's house, she found Naomi very excited. "What's the excitement?" asked Ruth. Naomi smiled and answered, "I have come to a decision. I am going home! I am packing my things, and I am going back to Bethlehem!" Ruth shook her head and said to her dear friend, "Naomi, I know you wish you were back home, but you are too old to travel there now. You can visit there in the stories you tell me and in your dreams at night." Naomi shook her head, "No, Ruth, you don't understand. Talking and dreaming about the little town is not the same as walking down the streets and smelling the smell that is the real Bethlehem. I must go home!"

Ruth understood and said, "It's clear you need to go, but you cannot travel alone. I will go with you." Naomi was amazed. She said to Ruth, "You can't come with me. You have a life here, a wonderful life and many friends." Naomi added, "Don't worry. I will be fine. I'm going home!" But Ruth shook her head, took Naomi's hands in hers, looked into her eyes and said,

♫ **Wherever you go, I will go too,**
'Cause you've got me, my friend,
And I've got you.

Naomi was amazed. She looked at Ruth. She could not believe what a friend she had. All Naomi could say was, "What?"

And Ruth told her again,

♫ **Wherever you go, I will go too,**
'Cause you've got me, my friend,
And I've got you.

Naomi cried. She knew the trip would be so much easier with Ruth by her side. Ruth helped Naomi pack. "If you want, we'll leave tomorrow." Naomi smiled and said, "I'd love that." Ruth went home to pack and when Naomi climbed into bed that night, Ruth's words still sang in her mind.

♫ **Wherever you go, I will go too,**
'Cause you've got me, my friend,
And I've got you.

They traveled together all the way to Bethlehem. There they found a small house to share. They had very little money and not much food, but they had each other, and Naomi was happy to be back.

Their house was next to a farmer's field, and Ruth noticed that the farm workers, as was the custom, left corn behind for people who might not have enough food. So every evening Ruth went into the farmer's field and gathered the corn left behind.

The farmer who owned the field was named Boaz. One evening he was looking out his window and saw Ruth gathering corn. He asked some of the workers who she was. They answered, "That is Ruth. She lives next door and takes care of the old woman, Naomi. Ruth gathers corn to share with Naomi." Boaz smiled, "That Ruth is a good friend." Then he added, "Leave more corn behind. Let's make it a little easier for her."

This did make it easier for Ruth, and one evening Boaz decided he would like to meet Ruth. So he joined her in the fields and helped her gather corn. He didn't tell her that he owned the fields. They just talked and talked as they gathered the left-behind corn. They both enjoyed the evening and Boaz asked Ruth if he could join her again the next evening. "Sure," said Ruth, "I'd like that."

After that, at dusk every evening Boaz helped Ruth gather corn. Ruth still did not know that Boaz was the farmer who owned the land. She just thought he was a kind man helping her and her friend, Naomi.

These warm shared evenings continued. Boaz was in love, and he wanted Ruth to know how he felt. "I want to be with you, Ruth," said Boaz, "And I want you to know

♫ **Wherever you go, I will go too,**
'Cause you've got me, my friend,
And I've got you.

Ruth felt the same way. They were in love and decided to get married. "Come," said Ruth, "We must tell Naomi."

Naomi was happy for Ruth. She was thrilled that her great friend had found a man like Boaz who loved her so much. Soon Ruth and Boaz were married, and they moved into his home. But they didn't go alone. They invited Naomi to live with them, for she was Ruth's dear friend.

AFTER THE STORY

And just like Ruth, at school we build friendships that go on and on and on. Let's sing, "You've Got Me."

STORY-TELLING TIPS

- Add details to show how Ruth is a good friend to everyone in the village. An example: "listens to her friends when they are worried or sad." These details can echo the children's experience with good friends at school.
- Add specifics of Naomi's girlhood memories—memories that will make the listening experience more vital for the children.
- Extend the time of Ruth and Boaz getting to know each other with a repeated phrase: "They talked and talked, talked and talked, gathered corn and talked."

ART NEEDS

- Ruth
- Naomi
- Boaz the farmer
- Corn on stalks

STORY SKELETON

- Ruth is a friend to everyone in village.
- Her special friend is an old woman, Naomi.
- Every evening Ruth visits Naomi.
- Naomi talks of her homeland, where she grew up—Bethlehem.
- Naomi decides to go back to Bethlehem.
- Ruth says that she'll go too.
- Naomi says, "No."
- Ruth says, "Wherever you go, I will go too."

Wherever You Go

(The Story of Ruth and Naomi)

Bill Gordh

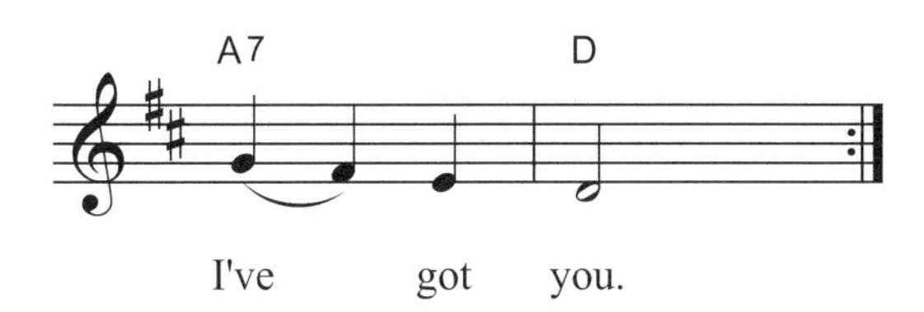

- Naomi can't believe it.
- Ruth tells her again.

♫

- Ruth helps Naomi pack.
- Naomi remembers.

♫

- They travel to Bethlehem.
- They find a small house.
- They see corn is left behind on the ground.

- Ruth collects corn each day for them to eat.
- The owner/farmer of the land is Boaz.
- Boaz sees Ruth collecting corn.
- Boaz joins Ruth collecting corn.
- Boaz and Ruth collect corn evening after evening.
- They work and talk.
- They fall in love.
- Boaz expresses his love.

♫

- They tell Naomi.
- Ruth and Boaz marry.
- Ruth and Boaz invite Naomi to move into Boaz's house with them.

chapter 13

JOSHUA AND THE CITY OF JERICHO
JOSHUA 6:1-20

A Story about Faith and Working Together

Sing-along "Joshua Fit the Battle Of Jericho"

The story of Joshua is an exciting one for children with the great walls of Jericho tumbling down. For older children it offers an interesting place to launch a discussion of some of the troubles that continue in the Middle East today. For younger children it provides a story illustrating the faith of Joshua and the power of a group of people working together.

BEFORE THE STORY

Today we are sharing the story of Joshua and the walled city of Jericho. The artwork is by _________ .

THE STORY

♫ *(sing-along)* **You've heard about the great King David.**
You've read about the wisdom of Saul.
But there's none like good old Joshua
And the Battle of Jericho.

Chorus **Joshua fit the Battle of Jericho, Jericho, Jericho.**
Joshua fit the Battle of Jericho
And the walls came a-tumblin' down.

This tale is about Joshua but we're not beginning the story with him. We are going back to Moses. You may remember that Moses led the people of Israel out of Egypt from lives spent in slavery and away from the Pharaoh who had treated them so terribly. Well, after they left, they began their journey to the Promised Land, a land God had said flowed with milk and honey. They traveled and traveled and traveled—day after day, week after week, year after year. They traveled so long that Moses died and they needed a new leader. They chose Joshua.

They asked Joshua what was next. They were tired of traveling. Joshua said to the Israelites that he was not sure, and when he was uncertain, he always prayed.

So Joshua went away.
And Joshua prayed,
And when he came back,
He had this to say,

"We must travel further. There is one more river to cross—the river of Jordan." That is what Joshua told the people and though they were tired of traveling they moved on. As they walked they chanted, "One more river, one more river to cross. One more river, one more river to cross." Finally they came to the river of Jordan. The people were excited. Finally—finally! But the river was swift and it looked like it would be hard to cross and some of the older people might not make it. What could they do?

They did not have to do a thing because suddenly the river stopped flowing! The waters were still and then they parted. The children of Israel walked across the dry riverbed, just like they had when they left Egypt across the Red Sea. After they crossed the Jordan, the river began to flow once more. The children of Israel were so excited, and they ran to the top of the hill to see the new land God had promised. They stopped. They couldn't believe what they saw. There was a city down in the valley. They didn't expect that! It was called Jericho and a huge wall surrounded the city. The Israelites looked at the great walled city. They saw soldiers standing along the top and peering through holes in the wall! It looked like the soldiers were ready to fight.

The people of Israel turned to Joshua. "What are we going to do? Those soldiers look like they are ready to fight." Joshua replied, "I'm not sure. I must pray."

So Joshua went away.
And Joshua prayed,
And when he came back,
He had this to say,

"We must march around the walled city for the next six days and never make a sound." The people scratched their heads. It sounded like a crazy idea. How could marching around a city do anything? But God had told Joshua, and they agreed to give it a try.

So on Day Number One:
March, march, march, march, march, march, march,
And they never made a sound.
Day Number Two:
March, march, march, march, march, march, march,
And they never made a sound.
Day Number Three:
March, march, march, march, march, march, march,
And they never made a sound.
Day Number Four:
March, march, march, march, march, march, march,
And they never made a sound.
Day Number Five:
March, march, march, march, march, march, march,
And they never made a sound.
Day Number Six:
March, march, march, march, march, march, march,
And they never made a sound.

At the end of Day Number Six they looked at the great walled city. It looked exactly the same. They said, "Joshua, we have done what you said, but nothing has happened. What do we do now?" Joshua said, "Let me pray."

So Joshua went away.
And Joshua prayed,
And when he came back,
He had this to say,

"Tomorrow is the seventh day and this time, it will be different. Bring your trumpets. Bring your ram horns and all your noisemakers. We will start by marching toward the city. Then I will tell you what to do." The next day they began.

♫ **Up to the walls of Jericho**
They marched right o'er the land.
Go blow those ram horns, Joshua cried,
For the battle is in God's hands.

And that's what they did. They marched, and they blew their horns. Then

♫ **Those old sheep horns began to blow.**
Trumpets began to sound.
Joshua commanded the children to shout . . .

At first the children did not make a noise. There were many children traveling with their families on this great journey, and they were marching right beside their parents. Joshua gave his command again

♫ **Joshua commanded the children to shout . . .**

This time they shouted. They shouted out all the noise that they had been holding in for the last six days and more. What a shout it was and with all those children shouting together, this is what happened

♫ **The walls came a tumbling down.**
Chorus **Joshua fit the Battle of Jericho, Jericho, Jericho**
Joshua fit the Battle of Jericho
And the walls came a-tumblin' down.
And the walls came a-tumblin' down.
And the walls came a-tumblin' down.

AFTER THE STORY

And that is the story of Joshua who did not give up, who kept his faith, and prayed when he needed help. Now we will sing the whole song of Joshua together.

STORY-TELLING TIPS

- There are a number of ways to include the traditional song within this story.
  - You can sing the parts or have a guest singer from your teaching staff or someone from one of your families as guest singer.
  - You can speak the lyrics as they have a rhyme and rhythm and will prepare the listeners to sing the song more fully during the sing-along after the story.
  - You can omit the song entirely and offer a spoken narrative describing the same events.
- For the "March, march, march" chant, speak in a very low almost whisper voice. This lets the children know that it was quiet but intense! The final "march" is underlined in the text to indicate the stress you put on the final sound of the line.
- When it comes time for the children to shout, if they don't call out loudly enough, stop the story and ask them to shout again. They love having permission to shout in this setting and are thrilled when the walls come tumbling down.

ART NEEDS

(We don't represent the people of Jericho, as this story is focused on Joshua and the children of Israel. The walled city itself becomes what they need to defeat.)

- Joshua
- The walled-city of Jericho
- A wall that can tumble down
- The Israelites (optional)
- The river of Jordan (optional)
- A ram's horn (optional)
- The Israelites (optional)

STORY SKELETON

♫

- Moses leads the Israelites out of Egypt.
- Moses dies.
- Joshua is new leader.
- The people ask Joshua, "When will we get to the Promised Land?"
- Joshua asks in prayer.
- They have one more river to cross.
- They finally reach Jordan and cross the river.
- They reach the top of the hill.
- They see the walled city of Jericho.
- They see soldiers ready to fight.
- The Israelites do not want to fight.
- Joshua goes to pray.
- God tells them to march around the city in silence for six mornings.
- On the seventh God tells them to march towards the walls and at the signal to make lots of noise.

♫

- The children shout!

♫

- The walls come tumbling down.

♫

chapter 14

JESUS CALLS HIS DISCIPLES

MATTHEW 9:9; MARK 1:14-20; LUKE 6:13; JOHN 1:43-45

A Story about Working Together

Sing-along "Work a Little Bit" (p. 242)

It's important for children to know that we respect the work they do and acknowledge that they have "great, big jobs." It is also helpful to point out that these big jobs often need more than one person. The story of Jesus realizing that he can use some help and seeking the helpers he needs is a good model for a child's everyday life.

This chapel begins with another Bible story, that of Jesus as a boy in the temple. This story demonstrates the significance of children thinking about what they will do when they grow up. The opening story about Jesus as a small boy may be used as a stand-alone chapel, although it would be a very short presentation.

BEFORE THE STORY

Today's story is really two stories from the Bible about Jesus. The first describes a time when Jesus was a boy, and the other is about Jesus when he is older and ready to begin his work. The art is by _______ .

THE STORY

Recently we talked about Jesus when he was a baby. Mary and Joseph had taken him to the great temple in Jerusalem. We heard the old man Simeon and the old woman Anna and the children sing their blessings to the baby. Well, babies get bigger and Jesus did too. He became a little boy. The Bible doesn't tell us many stories about Jesus as a boy, but there is one about a time Mary and Joseph thought he was lost.

The family had been to the temple. After the service, everyone left, and they were all walking and talking together. After a while Mary and Joseph called to Jesus. They figured he was walking behind them, but he wasn't there. They looked everywhere. They wondered if he was hiding. Finally they found him. He was still in the temple! They discovered him sitting with the grown-ups discussing the love of God.

Mary and Joseph came up to him, "We were so worried! We thought you were lost!" Jesus looked at them and smiled. He said, "There was no need to worry. We're talking about God and God's great love for all people. I told them that when I grow up I'm going to travel around and tell everyone about the love of God, about working together, and being like brothers and sisters in a world of peace." Mary and Joseph smiled. "That is a wonderful idea, but now it's time to go home!"

Time went by and when Jesus grew up, he remembered his childhood idea and went to his parents. He said, "I'm grown up now, and I want to travel and let everyone know about the love of God, tell stories about sharing and caring, and the importance of people being good neighbors. That's my plan."

Mary and Joseph nodded. They liked Jesus' plan, and it gave them an idea. They sang to Jesus.

♫ **You've got a great big job and a workin' plan,**
But you'll need some help to do it.

Jesus looked at them and thought about what they said.

♫ **You've got a great big job and a workin' plan,**
But you'll need some help to do it.

Jesus thought about what they suggested. Then he said, "You're right. The first thing I'll do is to find some good helpers, so we can work together!" So

He walked and walked,
Walked and walked and walked,
Walked and walked 'til he came to the sea.

There he saw four people fishing from a boat. Jesus stood on the shore watching. The fishing people stopped their fishing and without saying a word, set their sail for shore. The four friends jumped out of their boat and walked up to Jesus. Jesus looked at them and said, "I am traveling everywhere to tell people about the love of God, about sharing and caring and working together." Then he sang,

♫ **I've got a great big job with a workin' plan,**
And I need some help to do it.
So, won't you come with me,
Won't you come with me?

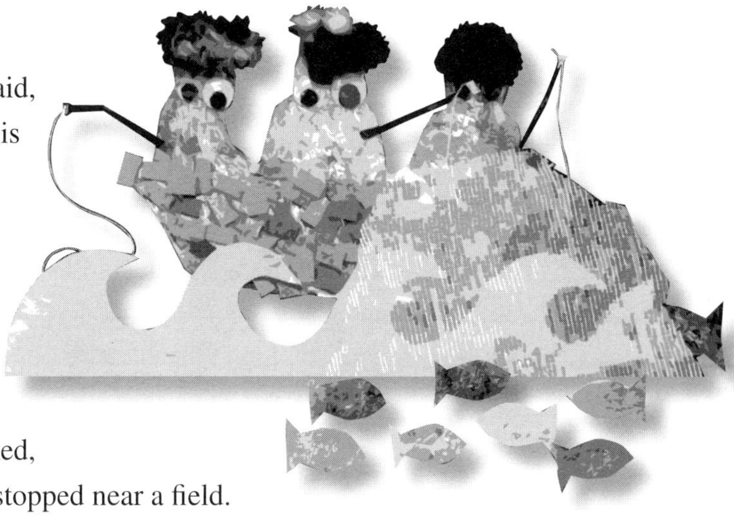

The people who had been fishing said, "We'd love to help you!" So Jesus counted his new friends

1, 2, 3, 4
I have four,
But we need some more.

And off they went. So

They walked and walked,
Walked and walked and walked,
Walked and walked 'til they stopped near a field.

There they saw four people cutting hay in the field. Jesus and his new friends stopped and watched the field-workers. The farm people stopped their work and without saying a word, put down their tools and went over to Jesus. Jesus looked at them and said, "I am traveling everywhere to tell people about the love of God, about sharing and caring and working together." Then he sang

♫ **I've got a great big job with a workin' plan,**
And I need some help to do it.
So, won't you come with me,
Won't you come with me?

The people who had been cutting hay said, "We'd love to help you!" So Jesus counted his new friends:

1, 2, 3, 4
5, 6, 7, 8
We have eight,
And that is great,
But we could use some more.

So

They walked and walked,
Walked and walked and walked,
Walked and walked 'til they came to the city.

There they stopped on a corner. When Jesus stopped, four people across the street stopped talking and walked across to Jesus and his eight helpers. Jesus looked at them and said, "I am traveling everywhere to tell people about the love of God, about sharing and caring and working together." Then he sang

♫ **I've got a great big job with a workin' plan,**
And I need some help to do it.
So, won't you come with me,
Won't you come with me?

The city friends answered Jesus, "We'd love to help you!" So Jesus counted his new friends:

1, 2, 3, 4
5, 6, 7, 8,
9, 10, 11, 12.
12!

"Twelve friends and there are twelve months in the year. I have help for all the year round!" declared Jesus.

And that is how Jesus got his helpers. We sometimes call them the disciples, and they had a song to sing!

♫ **We've got a great big job and a workin' plan**
And together we can do it.
Together we can do it.

AFTER THE STORY

And we've got a lot of great big jobs here at school and by working together, we get them done. The sing-along is "Work a Little Bit."

STORY-TELLING TIPS

- Have the children count the helpers with you each time. They enjoy counting and it further engages them in the story.
- The twelve helpers/disciples are placed in three groups of four to make the story simpler, as the point is getting people to help on a big important job.

The workers etc. are not identified as men, because for this story it is more important that there are people ready to help.

- If you use the Martin Luther King story (Chapter 31) about King as a child, and you use the disciple story after, you can refer to the King story and mention how Jesus also had a dream as a child about what he was going to do.
- If you have some associates to sing along, you can ask them to join in on the singing of the refrain once there are some disciples.

ART NEEDS

(Because of the brevity of the story, we generally don't use artwork for Jesus in the temple, and introduce the artwork for the disciples segment.)

- Jesus
- Four people fishing
- Four people farming
- Four people in the city

STORY SKELETON

- Jesus as a boy has spent the morning in the temple with Mary and Joseph.
- Everyone leaves the temple.
- After a while Mary and Joseph realize the Jesus is not with them or any of their friends.
- They find him at the temple.
- He tells them not to worry. He is just getting ready for his big job when he grows up.
- He is just talking with the elders about the love of God, people taking care of each other and making the world a peaceful place.
- Time goes by.
- Jesus is grown up and ready to leave home.
- He tells Mary and Joseph his plans for sharing the word of God.
- They tell him he may need some help for such a big job.

Great Big Job

(Jesus Calls His Disciples)

Bill Gordh

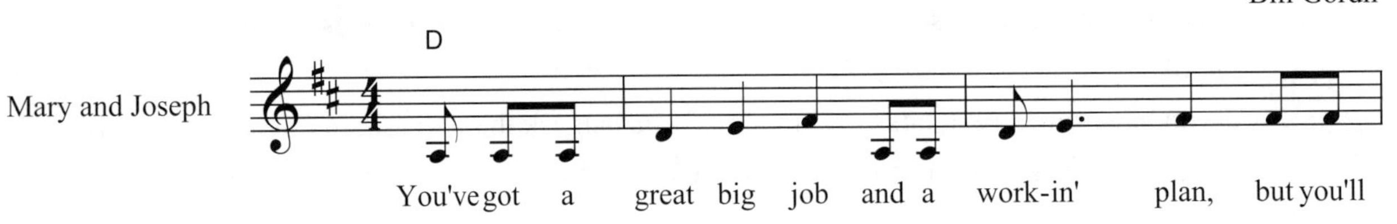

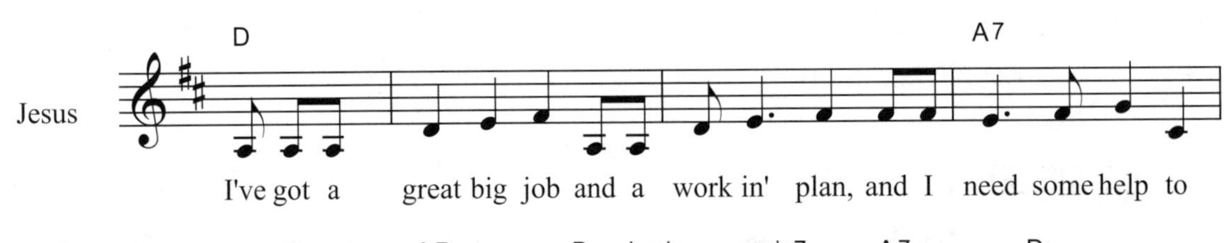

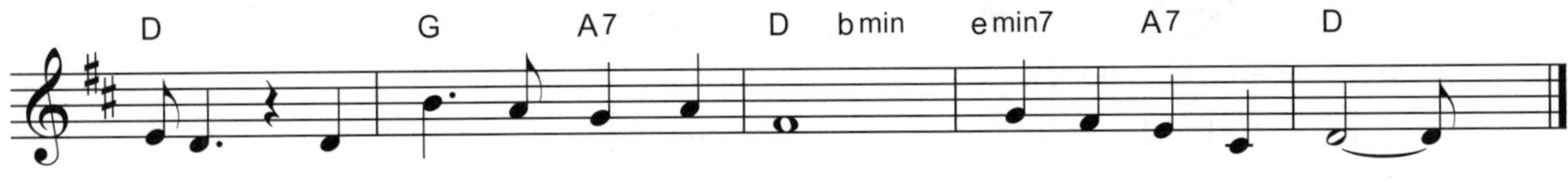

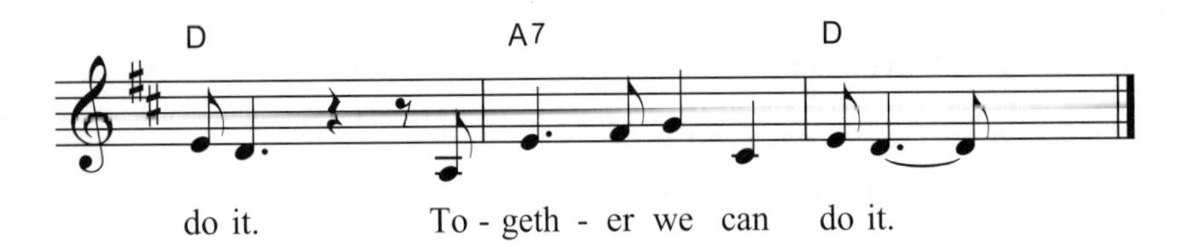

- He agrees and goes to find some helpers.
- He walks 'til he comes to the sea.
- Four fishermen stop fishing and come to shore.
- Jesus tells plans and asks them to join him.

♫

- They agree.
- They walk until they stop near a field.
- Four field-workers stop working and come to the road.
- Jesus tells his plans and asks them to join him.

♫

- They agree. Now there are eight.
- They walk until they come to the city.
- Four people come over.
- Jesus tells plans and asks them to join him.

♫

- They agree. Now there are twelve helpers/disciples.
- There's a big job they're sure can be done if they work together.

♫

chapter 15

THE LAME MAN WALKS
LUKE 5:17-26

A Story about Helping Each Other

Sing-along "You've Got Me" (p. 258)

The story of Jesus healing the lame man is another story of the great powers of the love of Jesus and his care of all people. For a setting of children of varied cultural backgrounds, it becomes a story of how friends take care of each other.

This story, like "Jesus Heals the Sick: A Story of Saying Thanks" (Chapter 7), requires some thinking about the children who will hear it and their parents' feelings. Some are not comfortable with a story of a miraculous healing especially if a child in the group has a condition that is unlikely to be resolved. The focus here is more on the friends' willingness to help than it is about the miracle, but it still calls for sensitivity to the issues that may arise.

BEFORE THE STORY

Today's story is about Jesus on his travels. It is also about a man who could not walk and his very good friends. The artwork is by ________ .

THE STORY

Jesus continued his travels with his disciples. Everywhere he went he spoke of the love of God, about being a good neighbor, and taking care of each other. His love for everyone brought people from near and far to hear his stories. Besides the stories Jesus told himself, there were stories *about* Jesus, and how his great love could make people well.

On the day of today's story, Jesus was inside someone's house discussing God with teachers and lawyers. The room was full, and there was a crowd surrounding the house. People stood in the doorway, and others leaned in the windows. Everyone was listening to the discussions.

On the other side of town lived a man who was paralyzed; he could not walk. The Bible does not tell his name or how he became this way, but it does say that his friends came to him with the news of Jesus. "Come, Liam (We'll call him Liam)," they said, "You've heard the stories about Jesus and the power of his love. Let's go see him!" The paralyzed man looked at his friends and thanked them. He said, "That's a good idea, but it is all the way across the village."

"That's all right," said his friends, "We will carry you." Liam looked at his friends, amazed at their readiness to help him. He had heard of Jesus, and he did wonder about the man so many were talking about. Jesus might not come to their village again for a long time. "Thank you. I'd love to go." So Liam's friends picked him up (bed and all!) and carried him through the door and down the road.

It was not a big village, and it never took long to run or walk from one end to the other, but carrying someone was a different matter. After a couple of blocks, Liam's friends needed to rest. They set down his bed, had a drink of water, and squatted next to Liam. "It's still a lot further to the house," said Liam, "Maybe we should just go back. Then you can go on your own and tell me later all that Jesus said." His friends shook their heads. "You should see Jesus yourself!" they said. So after a few more minutes of rest, they were on the way again.

They had to stop a few more times along the way, but Liam didn't ask them to turn around again. He knew what they would say, and he was growing more and more excited about seeing the man named Jesus. Finally, they arrived. There was a crowd, a big crowd, and the friends set Liam down again. Liam realized there was no way even such good friends could get him through all the people and into the crowded house. He suggested that they go back home. But they weren't listening to Liam; they were making a plan.

They lifted him again and Liam figured they were turning around, but they didn't. They hoisted the bed up on their shoulders and made their way through the crowd. When they got to the house, they did not try to barge through the door. Instead they carried him up the stairs on the outside of the house to the roof. When they got onto the roof, they began to remove roof tiles, and soon there was a hole in the roof and they could see Jesus below!

Jesus looked up; Liam looked down into his loving eyes. The next thing Liam knew he was being lowered down through the hole into the house. When the bed touched the floor, the friends watched from above as Jesus greeted him. "You have very loving friends," said Jesus. "Now feel the love of God." He put his hands on Liam's paralyzed legs. "Now stand up," said Jesus softly. Liam could not believe what he was hearing and feeling. He stood up. Tears filled his eyes and rolled down his cheeks as Jesus spoke again, "Now walk." Liam walked!

The crowd parted as Liam walked across the room. Liam turned to Jesus. "Thanks," he said, knowing how much he wanted to say but couldn't.

Liam's friends watched from the roof as Liam walked out of the house and through the crowd. They raced down the outside stairs and caught up with Liam. They walked together in silence back across town. Liam was thinking about miracles—the miracle of friendship and of the love of God.

AFTER THE STORY

We tell this story to remind ourselves of the importance of friendship and being ready to help friends who need us. Our sing-along is "You've Got Me."

STORY-TELLING TIPS

- The journey across the village is not described in the Bible but in this context makes more real the experience of the paralytic, and the choices his friends make to help him.
- Depending on the children, you may need to explain a tiled roof. The removal of the tiles suggests that they can be put back and avoids the image of these friends tearing a hole in someone's roof.

ART NEEDS

- The paralyzed man
- Friends
- Jesus
- Roof (optional)
- Crowd (optional)

STORY SKELETON

- Jesus comes to town.
- Friends gather around the paralyzed man, Liam.
- They tell him he should see Jesus.
- They say they will carry him.
- They carry him on his bed across town.
- It's hard work!
- They stop a few times to rest.
- They arrive at the house where Jesus is.
- There is a big crowd.
- There is no way to get the paralyzed man into the house through the crowd.
- The friends carry Liam up on the roof.
- They take tiles off the roof.
- They lower him down to Jesus.
- Jesus notes the loving care of Liam's friends.
- Jesus places his hands on the man's legs and tells the man to stand.
- Liam stands.
- Jesus tells the man to walk.
- He walks.
- He turns to say, "Thanks."
- His friends join him, and they all walk back together.
- Liam marvels at the miracle of friendship and of the love of God.

part 4

STORIES OF FAITH, NEW LIFE, AND CELEBRATION

chapter 16

DAVID AND GOLIATH
1 SAMUEL 17:1-52

A Story about Faith in God and the Power of Poetry and Song

Sing-along "You Can Sing about Anything" (p. 256-257)

In a time when we try to stay away from stories that suggest violence as a solution, the story of David and Goliath presents a challenging situation. One might choose other parts of David's life and tell about the composing of the Psalms and use the story to celebrate music, songs, creativity, and the greatness of God's love. But the story of David and Goliath is one that is already a part of the popular imagination, and small children have many "big giants" that need to be defeated. By taking on the story ourselves, we can underline the difficulty of David's choice to fight and the desire to return to the world of peace and music.

There are two suggestions for endings for this story. One closes with a psalm. The other ends with the children singing the "Little David" song. Both are effective endings, and you should choose the one that feels best for you and your group.

BEFORE THE STORY

Today's story from the Bible is about a boy named David, a shepherd boy who took care of the sheep and would one day be a great king. The artwork is by _______ .

THE STORY

Once there was a village, a very peaceful village where the people worked together, played, and prayed and sang together. Every morning the children gathered in the village and then all together ran out of the village and up the hill through the tall grass. And where were they running? They were running to find David. And why was

David on the hillside? He was on the hillside watching over the sheep for this was the young boy David's special job. And the sheep felt safe with David because he played music for them—music on his harp.

The children sang to David,

♫ **Little David, play on your harp, Hallelu, Hallelu.**
Little David, play on your harp, Hallelu.

And David played—his harp.

His music made the sheep feel safe and happy, and his music filled the valley and made the life there even more peaceful. And David not only played music; he also made up songs. He made up songs about everything that was in his heart and on his mind, everything he saw and heard and felt. He sang songs about the fields of green and the skies of blue. He sang songs about caring and sharing and singing and feeling safe. He sang songs of praise and prayer, of love and peace and laughter and all the things there are to see or feel or think about. He sang to God. He wrote songs about the love of God and how safe he felt knowing that he was loved.

This was a peaceful valley, but just over the hill was another village that was not peaceful at all.

For some reason, no one's quite sure why, the people in the other little village were always in a bad mood. They never had a good thing to say about anyone, so they always hurt each other's feelings. They argued back and forth, back and forth in this grouchy village, so no one was happy. What really drove them crazy was hearing David's beautiful music. You see, hearing that music would make almost anyone smile or feel a little better, but it only made these neighbors grouchier. They wanted David's music stopped.

In that grouchy little village lived a very big man. In fact, he was a giant, and his name was Goliath. He had an idea to save his town some trouble and make some trouble himself. He loved causing trouble. Goliath said he'd go personally over to the other village and stop the music. He was ready to fight anyone, and there would be no talking, no discussion at all, just fighting. He was a giant and a strong one at that, and he laughed at the idea of anyone trying to fight him.

He started walking up over the hill. With each step, the ground shook and it sounded like thunder. When the people in David's village saw the giant coming, they ran into their houses and locked the doors. At the same time, David was out in the fields playing his harp. He was looking up into the hills and thinking of God's love, "I lift my eyes to the hills. . . ." sang David. He felt the ground shake. He stopped his song. He listened. He did not hear what he usually heard: the sound of busy, happy people in his village. Something was wrong. David put down his harp, sent his sheep up the hill where they would be safe, and walked down into the village.

The village was silent. As David walked down the street, he saw his friends and neighbors peeking out their windows. Then David saw a shadow on the ground. It was a great big shadow. David followed the shadow to the feet of the Giant and on up, up, up to his face.

"I am Goliath, and I am ready to fight!" roared the giant.

"I am David, and I am ready to talk," replied David.

"Fight!" roared Goliath.

"Talk," said David.

"Fight!" roared Goliath.

"Talk," said David.

"Fight!" roared Goliath.

"Talk," said David.

This was already more talk than Goliath liked, so he shouted, "I'm going to stomp you into the ground, and stop that beautiful music forever!"

David looked up towards the hills that surrounded the village. He remembered his new song, "I will lift up my eyes. . . ." He felt the power of God's love. On the ground near his foot, David saw a smooth round stone. He quietly leaned over and picked it up. He fit it into the sling he used to scare animals away from his sheep. He spun the sling one, two, three times around and let it go. The stone sailed up, up, up through the air and hit the Giant in the center of his forehead. Goliath crashed to the ground.

The people ran out of their houses. They gathered around the fallen giant. They looked at each other.

"David saved us, David saved us!" they cried.

They looked around for David, but they didn't see him. Where could David be?

Ending One

A little girl cried out, "Listen!" Everyone listened. The beautiful music from David's harp came down from the hills. David was back with his sheep and his music and finishing the song he had started.

"I lift up my eyes to the hills
To find the help I need.
My help comes from the Lord—
True now and ever shall be."
AMEN

Ending Two

The children called out, "We know. Follow us!" The people of the village followed the children through the village and out into the fields, across the grass, and up the hill to where David sat watching over his sheep.

The children sang to David,

♫ **Little David, play on your harp, Hallelu, Hallelu.**
Little David, play on your harp, Hallelu.

And David played and played and played. He played about the love in his heart. He sang about his help in the hills, and how the love of God goes on and on and on.

AFTER THE STORY

And that is a story of David, a shepherd and songmaker. Now we'll sing "You Can Sing about Anything."

STORY-TELLING TIPS

- The song "Little David" can be accompanied by "slap and clap" of everyone. "Slap and clap" is when you clap your hands and then slap your thighs to a constant beat. Get the rhythm going first until everyone is doing it together. Then you can chant or sing the song to the rhythm of your clapping.
- The dialog between David and Goliath can be very effective using a seated colleague as David and the storyteller standing on a chair as Goliath. In that you have been praising David's music-making, the children will accept you being Goliath for a few moments and moving back into the narrator mode following the fall of Goliath.

ART NEEDS

- David
- Harp (optional)
- Goliath
- Sling (optional)
- Small stone (optional)
- Flock of sheep (optional)
- Group of children (optional)
- Rock for David to be on (optional)

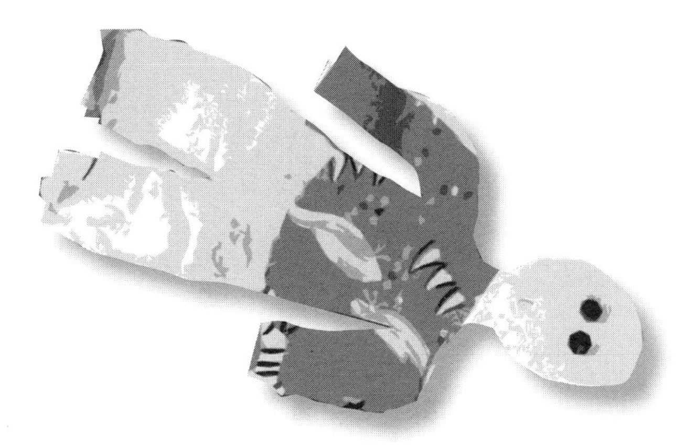

STORY SKELETON

- Peaceful valley and village.
- Shepherd boy David and his sheep.
- Children visit David and ask for his music.

♫

- David plays music and it fills the valley.
- In the village over the hill, the people are grouchy and always arguing.
- The grouchy people hate beautiful music.
- The giant Goliath goes to fight and stop the music.

- Goliath stomps into David's village.
- Everyone hides.
- David in the hills hears the silence in the village.
- David puts down his harp and walks into his village.
- David sees Goliath.
- Goliath wants to fight.
- David suggests that they talk.
- Goliath wants to fight and is about to hit David.
- David picks up stone and with his sling hurls the stone at Goliath.
- It hits Goliath in the forehead and Goliath crashes to the ground.
- David returns to the hills and his music and sheep.
- David finishes his song about how he feels God's love in the hills.

OR

- Children go and sing their David song and David plays.

♫

chapter 17

MOSES AND THE PHARAOH
EXODUS 3:1 – 12:30

A Story about Faith

Sing-along "Go Down, Moses"

The story of Moses and the Pharaoh is a long one and could easily take up more than one chapel. However, here we wish to present Moses' faith and desire for justice and God's love and protection of those people enslaved. The death of the first born is not mentioned in this story, but the word "passover" is used to demonstrate that all the plagues "passed over" the children of Israel. This gives young children a sense of the pass-over idea.

BEFORE THE STORY

This week we will share another story from the Bible—the story of Moses and the Pharaoh. The artwork is by ________ .

THE STORY

♫ **When Israel was in Egypt land . . .**

Long, long ago the people of Israel lived in Egypt. They had been there since the days of Joseph and his dreams. The Pharaoh during the time of Joseph had been a generous ruler, but the Pharaoh at the time of this story was mean and selfish. With this Pharaoh, the children of Israel were no longer happy being in Egypt, for they were slaves! Pharaoh made them work night and day, day and night—day after day after day, and they were never paid! They lived in a neighborhood in small houses and were only given enough food to keep them working, and work is all they ever did.

There was a young man living in the palace of Pharaoh, and his name was

Moses. He was a child of Israel but had grown up in Pharaoh's palace. He had a nice life, but he watched his people as slaves working day and night, night and day, and it made him very sad. Moses went to Pharaoh and said, "My people are slaves. It is a terrible life. Let me lead them away from Egypt." Pharaoh smiled, but shook his head, "Never! All their work makes me rich and powerful! I will never set them free."

Moses wandered out into the desert. There he saw a very strange thing, a burning bush. The bush was on fire, but the fire did not burn up the bush! Then a voice came from the bush. It was the voice of God! The voice said,

♫ **Go down, Moses**
Way down in Egypt land.
Tell old Pharaoh
To let my people go.

Moses could not believe what he heard. He said, "What?" and the voice repeated,

♫ **Go down, Moses**
Way down in Egypt land.
Tell old Pharaoh
To let my people go.

Moses looked at the bush and said, "I asked Pharaoh, but he just laughed and said, 'Never!'" The voice of God said, "Ask again and

♫ **Tell old Pharaoh**
To let my people go.

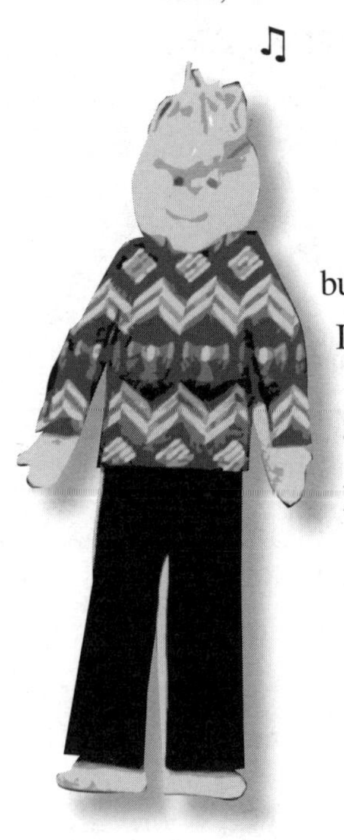

Moses asked, "But what if he doesn't listen?"

The voice answered, "I will be with you, Moses. You will not see me, but I will always be with you. When the time comes, if Pharaoh says, 'No,' I will speak to him in my own special way."

Moses traveled back to the palace and once again Pharaoh said, "Never!" Moses told him that God would speak to him in a special way. Pharaoh laughed.

But the next morning God spoke in a special way.
Rib-bit, Rib-bit! Pharaoh woke up.
There were frogs hopping 'cross his bed!
There were frogs at the door,

Frogs on the floor,

And a big frog on his head.

Pharaoh jumped out of bed and ran to the window. He looked outside. There were frogs all around the palace. Thousands of frogs hopping on houses, on people, on cats and dogs, but across town in the neighborhood of the people of Israel, there were no frogs at all! Back in the palace, there were frogs—more and more and more! They were driving Pharaoh crazy, until he called out, "Guards, bring Moses to me!" The guards brought in Moses. Pharaoh called to Moses, "Get rid of these frogs. If you do, I will let your people go!"

The frogs disappeared!!

Moses smiled, "Thank you, Pharaoh. I will go tell the people, and we will be gone before tomorrow." Moses walked across the room, but before he had taken five steps, Pharaoh said, "Oh Moses, now that the frogs are gone, I've changed my mind. In fact, the slaves must work harder today to make up for the frogs!" Moses was sad. He looked at Pharaoh, "God said that he is with me, that you should let us go. More things will happen. God will make them happen." Pharaoh laughed.

But then

Thump! Thump! Pharaoh looked out.

There was hail crashing on the ground.

Hail blew through the window

Slammed into Pharaoh

And his head was spinning 'round.

Pharaoh ran to the window. He watched the hail making holes in roofs and knocking people to the ground. But in the neighborhood of the children of Israel, Pharaoh saw that it was not hailing at all. It has passed over their neighborhood. Back at the palace, the sound of the hail smashing into everything was too much. Pharaoh once again called for Moses. The guards brought him in,

"Moses," cried Pharaoh, "Get God to stop this hail, and I will let your people go!" The hail stopped. It was quiet. The sun came out, and it was a blue-sky day. Moses smiled. "I will go tell my people. Then we will begin our journey to the land flowing with milk and honey that God told us about."

But before Moses had taken four steps, Pharaoh thought about what he had just promised and stopped Moses, "Never mind Moses, I've changed my mind. Your people will stay slaves forever, and forever making me richer and richer!" "Are you sure?" asked Moses. "I'm sure," answered Pharaoh.

Bzzz-Bzzz What is that?
Bugs were bugging Pharaoh now.
They made him itch
Wondering what is which,
And how can he end this—how?!

The bugs really drove Pharaoh wild, and when he looked outside, he saw everyone walking near the palace flicking away insects. The dogs and cats and cows and goats were scratching too, but over in the neighborhood where the people of Israel lived, it was peaceful—no bugs at all. The bugs had passed over the Israelite's neighborhood. Back in the palace, it was an itchy place. "Bring me Moses!" screeched Pharaoh, and the guards brought in Moses. "Get rid of these bugs, and I will let your people go!" The bugs disappeared. But once again the Pharaoh changed his mind.

And more plagues came—locusts swarmed in and ate all the leaves on all the trees and all the crops. Many more terrible things occurred and the Bible describes them all. Then one day, in the middle of the day, it was nighttime—well, dark as night anyway! Pharaoh stumbled over to the window in the darkness and looked outside. Darkness surrounded the palace, but the darkness had passed over the neighborhood of the people of Israel, and there was light there. Pharaoh was frightened. He called for Moses and in the dark they talked, and this time Pharaoh promised.

And soon Moses and the people of Israel were leaving Egypt. That is the story of Moses and Pharaoh and some of the story of the Passover.

AFTER THE STORY

And Moses never lost faith. Now we'll sing, "Go Down, Moses."

STORY-TELLING TIPS

- You may want to have one or more singers sing the traditional "Go Down Moses" refrain during the story. It will add a nice dynamic. Alternatively, you can sing it, read it, or just describe what Moses was told.

- The poems are there to lighten the idea of the plagues while still presenting the story. The children think the frogs hopping on Pharaoh is funny, but they also understand what is happening. If you like the little poems that describe three of the plagues, you can memorize them or write them on a big card to let the children listeners know that you are reading this part of the story. Then you can tell the rest.
- Gesture to the back of the room as being where the children of Israel live at the beginning of the story. Another gesture is made to the back when describing that frogs and hail and bugs had passed over the Israelites. Then when the darkness comes, have one of the teachers turn out the lights in the front half of the room and leave on the lights in the back. It is very effective.
- You will want to adjust the speed of your story when talking about the frogs and hail and bugs to allow for the time it takes to place and remove the artwork.

ART NEEDS

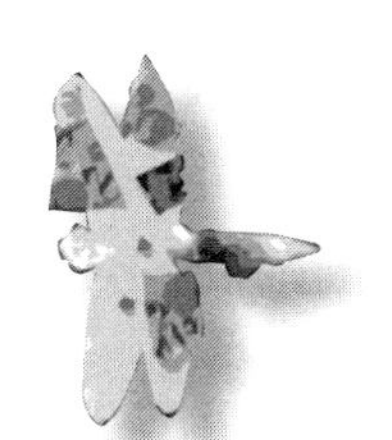

- Moses
- Pharaoh
- Burning bush (optional)
- Frogs
- Hail
- Bugs

STORY SKELETON

♫

- New Pharaoh is mean.
- People of Israel who live in Egypt since the days of Joseph are now slaves.
- As slaves they work all the time and have no money.
- They live in little houses on the outskirts of the city.
- Moses is an Israelite who grew up in the Pharaoh's palace.
- Moses sees how badly his people are treated.
- Moses asks Pharaoh if he (Moses) can lead the people away.
- Pharaoh says, "No!"

- Moses walks out into the desert.
- The voice of God speaks through a burning bush to Moses.

♫ "Let my people go."

- Moses says he tried already.

♫ "Tell old Pharaoh . . ."

- God says he will be with Moses and make Pharaoh understand.
- Moses goes and asks Pharaoh again.
- Pharaoh says, "No."
- Moses tells Pharaoh that God will speak in many ways.
- Pharaoh laughs.
- The frogs come. Lots and lots of frogs.
- No frogs where the Israelites live.
- Pharaoh calls Moses.
- Pharaoh says he'll let the people go if Moses gets rid of the frogs.
- The frogs are gone.
- Pharaoh changes his mind. People can't go!
- Hail falls.
- No hail on the children of Israel.
- Pharaoh calls Moses.
- Pharaoh says he'll let people go if the hail stops.
- The hail stops.
- Pharaoh changes his mind. People can't go!
- The bugs come.
- No bugs with the people of Israel.
- Pharaoh calls in Moses.
- Pharaoh says he will let them go if bugs are gone.
- The bugs disappear.
- Pharaoh changes his minds again. People can't go!
- This continues to happen through more plagues.
- Finally darkness passes over the children of Israel and plunges Pharaoh into blackness.
- Moses is finally able to lead the children of Israel out of Egypt.

chapter 18

DANIEL IN THE LION'S DEN
DANIEL 6:1-28

A Story about Faith

Sing-along "Daniel in the Lion's Den"

The story of Daniel gives us the opportunity to share a story about a man with a profound faith in God and the power of prayer. The story can be used to offer a model for prayer, pointing out the opportunity to express all of what one is thinking and feeling. The story also presents Daniel as someone grateful for his life and those around him. His gratitude is expressed in the refrain, "I want to thank you."

The story has been simplified to point out and compare two dual relationships: Daniel and the king, and Daniel and God. This story choice leads the children listeners to focus on Daniel's dilemma.

BEFORE THE STORY

Today we are sharing a story from the Bible. It is about a man named Daniel who always took time for prayer. The artwork is by _______ .

THE STORY

Long ago there was a man named Daniel. He was a kind and generous friend and a hard worker. He had a job for the king, and he did his work with care. There was something else very important in Daniel's life in addition to his friends, his king, and his work. That was his faith in God. In fact Daniel talked to God every day when he prayed.

He prayed three times every day. He began each day with a prayer, a simple thanks for the chance to live another day trying to do his best. At lunchtime before he took a bite, he prayed again, "Thank you God for the food I'm about to eat." At the end of the day, he prayed again. His nighttime prayer was the most special of all, for then Daniel talked to God about everything that was on his mind and in his heart. He always closed with a little song.

♫ *Chorus* **I want to thank you**
For the things that you do.
I want to thank you again and again.
I want to thank you
For the love in my heart
And thank you for being my friend.

That is how it was day after day. A prayer in the morning before he went to work, a prayer before lunch to thank God for the food he was about to eat, and his long prayer at the end of the day. To close his prayer he always sang:

♫ *Chorus* **I want to thank you**
For the things that you do.
I want to thank you again and again.
I want to thank you
For the love in my heart
And thank you for being my friend.

Now Daniel liked to work for the king, and because he was kind and generous and a very good worker, the king noticed Daniel. They became very close friends. They talked about all kinds of things. One day Daniel was telling the king how much everyone loved him. The king asked Daniel how he knew. Daniel answered, "King, you should go and talk to the people. You will see for yourself." The king thought it was a good idea.

The next day, the king walked through the village and watched people at their work and play. He stopped and talked. He played with some children. At lunchtime, everyone went home. The king walked down the quiet street. He looked into a window. There he saw a family saying a prayer before lunch, "Thank you, God, for the food we're about to eat." The King smiled and walked on. The next house was the same. There was another family with heads bowed, "Thank you, God, for the food we're about to eat." The king smiled and moved on. Each house was the same, and the king reached Daniel's house. He listened, "Thank you, God, for the food I'm about to eat." The king smiled and started walking back home, happy to have spent the morning with his people.

As he walked, the king started thinking, "The people are all praying to God for their food. But really I'm the one who makes their lives so good. Without me, what would they do? The people should be praying to me, the king and not to God!" The king liked this idea and decided it should be the law. He called together his guards and told them to travel across the kingdom announcing, "From now on, no one may pray to God. Everyone must pray to the king!" The guards looked at the king and asked, "Really?" "Really!" declared the king. One of the guards then asked, "But King, what will you do if someone prays to God?" The king thought for a moment and then declared, "If anyone dares pray to God, he or she will be thrown into a den of hungry lions!"

Well, the word went out, and soon everyone was praying to the king, every-one—except Daniel. The king decided to take a walk down the same street at lunchtime to find out how his law was working. He wanted to hear the prayers. He stopped near the open window of a house where the family was sitting down for lunch. He heard, "Thank you, King, for the food we are about to eat." The king smiled and walked on. At the next house he heard, "Thank you, King, for the food we are about to eat." He smiled. House after house he heard the same prayer, "Thank you, King, for the food we are about to eat." Then he stopped at Daniel's house. He listened, "Thank you, God, for the food I am about to eat." The king could not believe it! Daniel, his good friend Dan-iel, was still praying to God! The king made some noise outside so that Daniel would know he was listening. The king hoped Daniel would change his prayer. Daniel began his prayer again, "Thank you, God, for the food I am about to eat."

The king called his guards, and they knocked on Daniel's door. Daniel opened the door. The king cried out, "Daniel, you are still praying to God! Don't you know the new law? You are supposed to pray to me!!" Daniel smiled and answered, "King, you are a great king, but you are not God. You did not make this world. You do not make the sun shine or the wind blow or the rain fall or fill my heart with love. I can never pray to a person. I will only pray to God." The king shook his head and said, "But Daniel, do you know the punishment?"

"Yes," said Daniel. "Very well," said the king. "Guards, throw Daniel into the den of hungry lions!" The guards took Daniel away, and the king went back to his palace. Daniel was thrown into the den of hungry lions, and the king went to bed. But he did not sleep. He could not sleep. He felt terrible. Daniel was a friend. The king lay awake until the sun came up. Then he ran to the lions' den, expecting to see a pile of bones. But there was Daniel, and he was alive and well! In fact he was petting the lions as though they were kitty cats! "Thank God!" exclaimed the king. "Exactly," replied Daniel, "Thank God." "But why are you alive?" asked the king. "Prayer," said Daniel. "Prayer?" asked the king. "Yes," said Daniel, "I prayed to God to protect me from the hungry lions and he heard my prayer."

The king hugged Daniel, turned to his guards and announced, "I am king, and I am a king who made a mistake. So I will change the law. From now on no one may pray to me, only to God, only to God."

And so life returned to normal in the village where Daniel lived. Then one morning just as Daniel knelt down to pray, he heard a knock on his door. It was the king! "Is something wrong?" asked Daniel. "No," said the king, "I have come to pray with you."

And so Daniel and the king prayed together. At the close of their prayer they sang:

♫ *Chorus* **I want to thank you**
For the things that you do.
I want to thank you again and again.
I want to thank you
For the love in my heart
And thank you for being my friend.

AFTER THE STORY

And that is the story of Daniel, a man who never lost faith, and who always remembered to say, "Thank you." Let's all sing "Daniel in the Lion's Den."

STORY-TELLING TIPS

- Use your own feelings about prayer to describe Daniel's.
- Pause each time at the end of the little prayer, "Thank you, God, for the food I'm about to eat." You might even "ping" a chime as an accent at the end of the prayer. When people are praying to the king, this same pause allows this change in prayer to really sink into the young listener.

ART NEEDS

- Daniel
- King
- Lion's den
- Lions

STORY SKELETON

- Daniel prays three times a day.
- At lunch: "Thank you, God, for the food I'm about to eat."
- At night he always closes his prayer with "Thank you" song.

I Want to Thank You (Refrain)

(The Story of Daniel)

Bill Gordh

- Always the same, morning, noon, and night.

♫

- Daniel works for the king.
- Daniel is an excellent worker and a faithful friend.
- Daniel and the king become friends.
- The king goes out to find out what the people think about him.
- King walks down the village street at lunchtime.
- Everyone at lunch: "Thank you, God, for the food I'm about to eat."
- Last house is Daniel: "Thank you, God, for the food I'm about to eat."
- On walk home, king thinks about how he feels he is the reason people are happy, not God.

- King decides people should pray to him, the king, instead of God.
- King makes new law: "Pray to king. Do not pray to God."
- King orders guards to spread the word.
- Guards are surprised and ask what happens if someone prays to God anyway.
- The king says that person will be tossed into the den of hungry lions!
- King walks down street.
- Everyone at lunch: "Thank you, King, for the food I'm about to eat."
- King smiles.
- Last house is Daniel: "Thank you, God, for the food I'm about to eat."
- King cannot believe it. Makes noise and listens.
- Daniel: "Thank you, God, for the food I'm about to eat."
- King, "Why Daniel?"
- Daniel, "You are a great king, but you are not God. I cannot pray to a person."
- Daniel to the lions. King to the palace.
- King can't sleep.
- In morning king runs to den.
- Daniel is fine.
- King says, "Thank God."
- Daniel says, "Exactly!'
- King changes law.
- King prays with Daniel.

♫

chapter 19

THE CHRISTMAS STORY

LUKE 1:26-38; 2:1-8

A story about Celebration of the Room for Us All in the Love of God

Sing-along "Silent Night"

The focus of this telling of the Christmas story is on Joseph and Mary trying to find a room for the birth of baby Jesus. The reason for this choice is to set up the ending where we point out that there is room for everyone in the love of God.

BEFORE THE STORY

Today's we get to share the Christmas story. The artwork is by _______ .

THE STORY

Over two thousand years ago, there was a woman named Mary. One day Mary heard fluttering in the sky, fluttering of wings. She looked up, and there she saw an angel. Most people never see an angel in their entire lives, and Mary never had either, so Mary was afraid. But the angel was kind and spoke to her, "Don't be afraid, Mary. You are a blessed woman. You are going to have a baby—the child of God!" Mary was still a little scared and very surprised. "I am?" she said. "You are," said the angel whose name was Gabriel. "Your son will be a prince, the Prince of Peace, and he will teach the world about sharing and caring and the love of God."

Mary smiled and shook her head. "That is not possible," she said. "I cannot have a prince. I am just an ordinary woman, and my husband, Joseph is a carpenter." "You will see," said Gabriel. "Your babe shall be the King of Kings, the Prince of Peace, and you shall name him, 'Jesus.'" The angel Gabriel flew up, up and away—he was gone. Mary was amazed and ran and told Joseph. Joseph hugged Mary and said, "We must take special care of you in the months to come, for we have been given a blessed job to do for God."

The months went by, and it was nearing time for the baby to be born. Joseph came to Mary with news he had just heard. "Mary, we must pack. It is a new law that we must return to the town where we were born to be counted." "Oh, Joseph," said Mary. "I can't travel now. The baby will soon be born." "We must both go. That is the law," replied Joseph. Mary shook her head. "But I can never walk all the way to Bethlehem," she said. "I am not strong enough!" Joseph replied. "You can ride on our donkey, the wonderful donkey, all shaggy and brown."

So soon, they were on their way to the little town of Bethlehem. In those days there were no planes, no cars or buses, so everyone traveled along the dirt roads that crossed the countryside. There were many people on the road as Joseph and Mary traveled. Some walked. Some were on donkeys, and still others rode on camels. They traveled and traveled. One evening they came over the hill and there lay the little town of Bethlehem. It was evening and there were candles flickering in the windows. Mary was tired. "We're almost there, "said Joseph. "We will find a place, an inn to stay in, and you can rest." "Good," said Mary. "I can feel that the baby is almost ready to be born." They traveled down the hill, past the farm where Boaz and Ruth and Naomi once lived, and they stopped before an inn.

Joseph went up the path and knocked on the door of the inn. KNOCK-KNOCK-KNOCK. The innkeeper answered the door. Joseph spoke, "My wife Mary is about to have a baby, and we need a place. May we have a room, please?" The innkeeper shook her head and said,

♫ **No room, no room,**
No room at all!

Joseph returned to Mary, "There's no room in the inn, but perhaps the next one." They stopped again. Joseph hurried up the path and knocked. KNOCK-KNOCK-KNOCK. The innkeeper answered the door. "Mary is going to have her baby. May we have a room?" But once again the innkeeper shook his head and said,

♫ **No room, no room,**
No room at all!

Joseph returned to Mary, "There's no room in that inn either, but I'm sure the next." But one after another the knocks were answered with a shaking head and the same refrain.

♫ **No room, no room,**
No room at all!

Mary was exhausted. She needed a place to rest, to sleep, to have her baby. There was one last inn. Joseph hurried to the door and knocked. KNOCK-KNOCK-KNOCK. "Yes?" said the innkeeper. "My wife Mary is about to have her baby, and we've been trying to find a place, but all the inns are filled. Do you have a room, PLEASE!?" But the kind innkeeper just shook her head and said,

♫ **No room, no room,**
No room at all!

Joseph started down the path, when he heard the voice of the innkeeper. "Wait. I have an idea,

♫ **In back**
There is a little stall.

"A stall, a stable for our baby?" The innkeeper nodded. Joseph called back, "Thank you" and hurried to Mary. "We have a place. It's not a room, but we can stay in the stable in the back." "A stable for a king?" murmured Mary. She smiled at the funny idea of a stable being the birthplace for the King of Kings, the Prince of Peace.

But when they got to the stable, it was peaceful. The cow moved aside to allow Mary and Joseph to use her manger for a cradle. The sheep and lambs were nearby. The doves were cooing in the rafters. Joseph hugged Mary. Mary looked up into the nighttime sky and there she saw a star, the most amazing bright star she had ever seen. It seemed to be shining down right on the stable. It's wondrous light spread across the fields and pastures for miles and miles and miles.

"Look, Joseph! The star. It is time for little Jesus to be born. There is the light, the love of God!"

And there in the stable the Prince of Peace was born, the boy who would grow up to teach the world about sharing and caring. The love of God like the light from the star shines on everyone in the world.

For in the love of God
There is room for us all.

♫ Everyone sings "Silent Night."

AFTER THE STORY

And at this time of year we always celebrate the birth of the little baby Jesus in Bethlehem, and we hope and pray for peace on earth and good will to all.

STORY-TELLING TIPS

- When Joseph and Mary are traveling, use the same lilting rhythm you used when Joseph (coat of many colors) traveled to Egypt. Using similar rhythms in your different stories help the young listeners join the story and also ties together some of the themes of the tales.
- Consider using different colleagues to be the innkeepers and answer Joseph's query with the refrain, "No room at all." I have found that teachers are flattered to be part of the stories, and the children love to see their teachers participate. It makes the story more personal for them.

ART NEEDS

- Angel (optional)
- Joseph
- Mary
- Donkey (optional)
- Stable
- Manger
- Baby Jesus

STORY SKELETON

- The angel Gabriel comes to Mary.
- He tells her she will have a baby.
- The baby will be the child of God and teach the world about sharing and caring and the love of God.
- Mary tells Joseph.
- Times goes by.
- Joseph tells Mary they must go to Bethlehem, their birthplace, to be counted in the census.
- Mary rides on the donkey as Joseph walks.
- They travel and travel.
- They approach Bethlehem.
- They need a place to stay, an inn.
- Joseph goes to the door of the inn and asks for a room.

No Room at All

(Christmas Story)

Bill Gordh

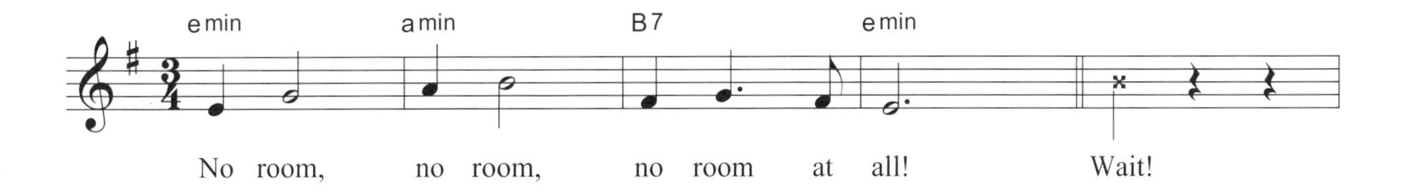

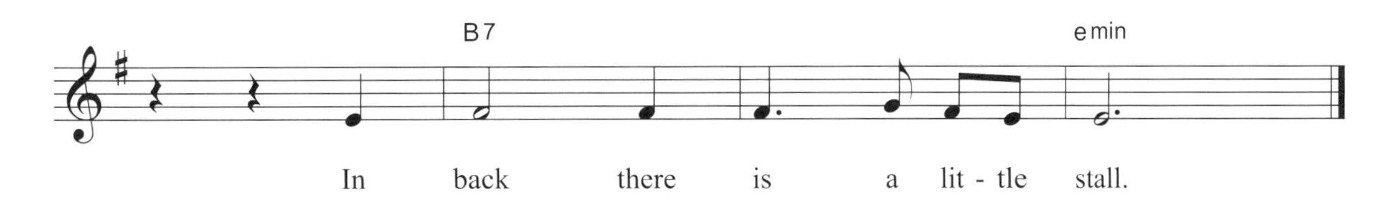

- They go to the next inn.

♫

- They try again and again.

♫

- Finally one last inn. Mary is ready to have her baby.

♫

- Joseph turns away.
- The innkeeper calls out, ♫ "In the back . . ."
- Mary smiles at the idea of a prince being born in a stable.
- Baby Jesus is born and laid in a manger.
- A great star shines down, representing God's love.
- The star shines down on all the world to remind us that in God's love, there is room for us all.

♫ "Silent Night"

chapter 20

BLESSINGS FOR BABY JESUS
LUKE 2:22-39

A Story of Celebration and Hope for Our Children

Sing-along "Love Begins with Giving" (p. 240-241)

This is very brief story one can tell soon after the children have come back from winter (Christmas) break. It is a gentle start for the new year. The children hear the blessings for Jesus, and it reminds them of that warm wonderful feeling of being a "Blessed Baby." We schedule our monthly birthday celebration to close this chapel.

BEFORE THE STORY

This is a story from the Bible about two old people, Simeon and Anna, and their blessings for baby Jesus. The artwork is by _________ .

THE STORY

Soon after baby Jesus was born, Mary and Joseph left the little town of Bethlehem and returned to their home in Nazareth. It was the custom at the time to take newborn children to the temple in Jerusalem for special services. So Mary and Joseph took baby Jesus to the great temple on the hill in Jerusalem—the temple where the first Hanukkah occurred. There they would hear prayers and see the lamp where the flame reminds everyone of God's love and how it goes on and on and on forever.

When they arrived, an old man named Simeon entered the temple and saw the baby Jesus. His face lit up. The old man was filled with joy. Mary looked at the old man and asked, "Why are you so happy?" "Well," replied Simeon, "this baby has been in my dreams. Night after night, I have dreamed of a child who would come to this earth and grow up to teach the world about peace and sharing and caring and the love of God.

When I saw Jesus, I knew he was that baby. May I hold him and give him my blessing?"

Mary answered, "Yes," and placed baby Jesus into the arms of the old man. The old man sang

♫ **Blest be the child**
Born of Mary!
Blessed be the smile
That crosses his face!
May he please lead us
To the peace that is needed,
And love fill the world
With God's given grace!

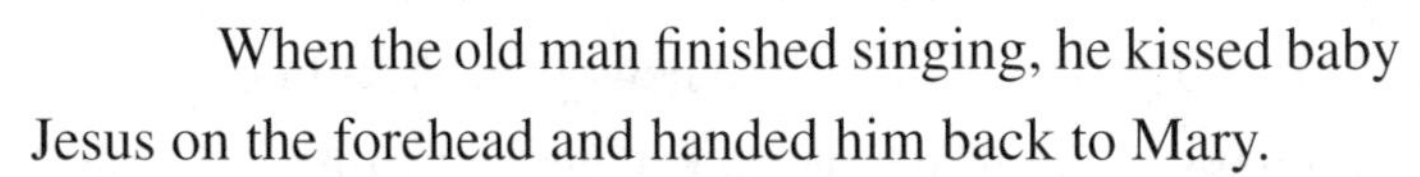

When the old man finished singing, he kissed baby Jesus on the forehead and handed him back to Mary.

Soon after an old woman named Anna came up. She spent most of her time in the temple praying and thinking. She was a prophetess and knew things that would happen in the future. When she saw baby Jesus, she was overjoyed. She knew that he would be a great teacher. She asked if she could hold the baby and give her blessing. Mary agreed and handed Jesus to Anna. The old woman sang her blessing.

♫ **Blessed be this little one!**
Pray for this little one!
Grow big, little one!
Teach us, little one,
To love, to love,
To love!

After her blessing, Anna handed Jesus back to Mary and moved back into the temple.

There were children in the temple and they gathered around the new baby. They too wanted to give their blessings, and the children were able to say what they felt with just two special words. They sang:

♫ **Blessed baby!**
Blessed baby!

Now sing all three parts (Simeon, Anna, and children) at once.

And that is the story of the blessings for the baby Jesus.

AFTER THE STORY

You know when you were all babies, your mothers and fathers had dreams and hopes for you. They still do! A hope and dream that you will all be blessed with good friends and loving families, and that you will learn to share and care for others. We'll sing "Love Begins with Giving."

STORY-TELLING TIPS

- The songs in this story are set up for at least two singers (you can be one of them), and one person to lead the listeners singing "Blessed baby!" However, the story is also very effective with the songs spoken or with one person singing Simeon and Anna's songs. After teaching the children the "Blessed baby" chorus, have them sing over and over as you or a colleague sing or speak the two blessing songs consecutively.

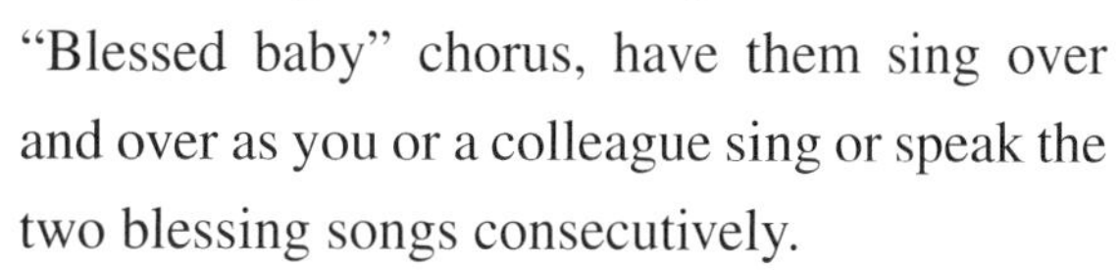

- You can spend more time talking about Simeon and Anna, though you want to keep the children's focus on baby Jesus.
- You may wish to create your own blessings and substitute them for the songs offered here.

ART NEEDS

- Joseph
- Mary
- Baby Jesus
- Old man
- Old woman
- Temple lamp with flame (This reminds the children of the Hanukkah story.)

STORY SKELETON

- Mary and Joseph bring baby Jesus to Jerusalem temple for blessings.
- Old man Simeon sees Jesus.
- Simeon has dreamed of a baby who will bring peace to the world.
- Simeon says/sings his blessing.

Blest Be the Child

(Simeon and Anna)

Bill Gordh

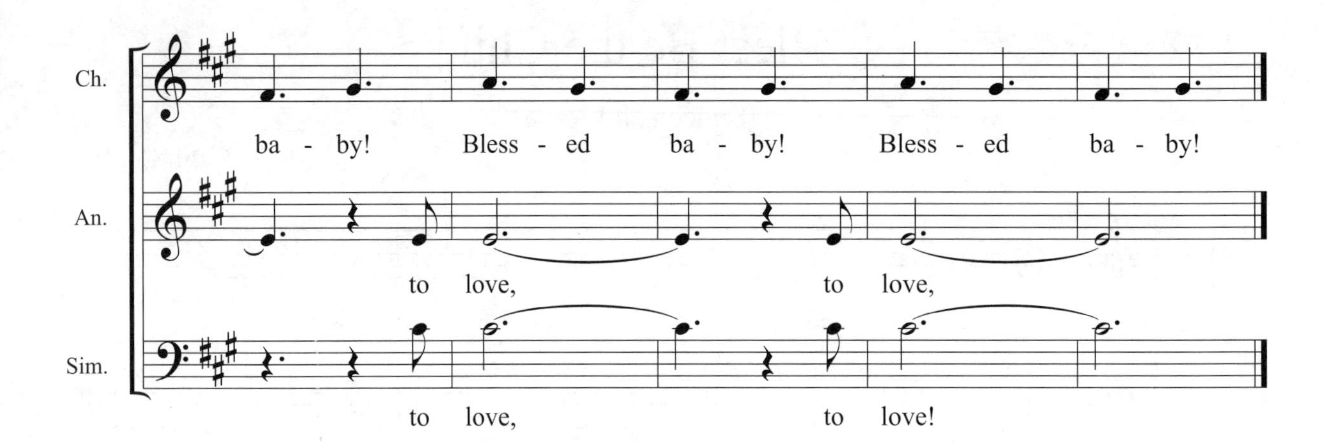

- Prophetess Anna see baby Jesus.
- She knows Jesus will be a great teacher.
- Anna holds Jesus.

♫

- Children gather around Jesus.
- They sing their blessing.

♫

- The three blessings are repeated together.

chapter 21

THE LAST SUPPER AND THE FIRST EASTER
LUKE 22:7-27

A Story about Faith and Carrying On

Sing-along "Love Begins with Giving" (p. 240-241)

In a chapel with children from a variety of religious backgrounds, the Last Supper and Easter pose a challenge to create a meaningful gathering for everyone attending. The considerations that have directed the inclusion of the rest of the stories in this book give us guidance here. We wish to use the stories to support the aims of taking care of each other and making the world a better place. Therefore, the crucifixion is not part of the story offered here, nor is the ascension. What is presented is that Jesus will die and that when he does, he lives on in our hearts and actions. The central focus is the Last Supper, with a gathering where Jesus prepares his helpers for what will come to pass. The story also has the disciples ask, "What will we do?" to parallel a child's natural response to the possibility of a great loss, "What happens to me?"

BEFORE THE STORY

Today we will share a story of the Last Supper and the first Easter. The artwork is by _______ .

THE STORY

Last week we told the story of Moses and how he led the people of Israel out of Egypt where they were slaves. Every year since the time of that exodus from Egypt, the children of Israel have celebrated Passover.

Now we go to the time of Jesus and his disciples traveling from town to town talking about the love of God, sharing and caring, working together, and being a good neighbor. Some of the time Jesus and the disciples traveled together, and at other times they split up. It was the time of the Passover, and Jesus called the disciples together to celebrate the annual Passover feast. When they all gathered around the table, Jesus broke the bread and passed it around. Then he thanked the disciples for their service, and he said, "This is our last supper."

The table was silent. The disciples stared at Jesus, "What do you mean, our last supper?" Jesus looked around the table and said, "Soon I shall die." The disciples looked at Jesus in disbelief. "But why?" they asked. Jesus answered, "There are people who do not like me. They do not like what I am trying to do." The disciples could not believe what they were hearing. They asked, "But what will we do without you?" Jesus smiled, "You will go on with the work we have begun. You will speak of God's love and you will tell the stories."

"What stories?" asked the disciples.

Jesus answered, "All the stories I tell. You can share the story of the shepherd who went searching for the one lost sheep, the story of the generous girl who shared her lunch of fish and loaves. You can tell the story of the farmer who gave the seeds to the children—the boy and girl dropped seeds along the path, and on the rocky ground and amongst the briers. Then they found how to make them grow—with loving care in the richest soil they could find. You can tell the story of

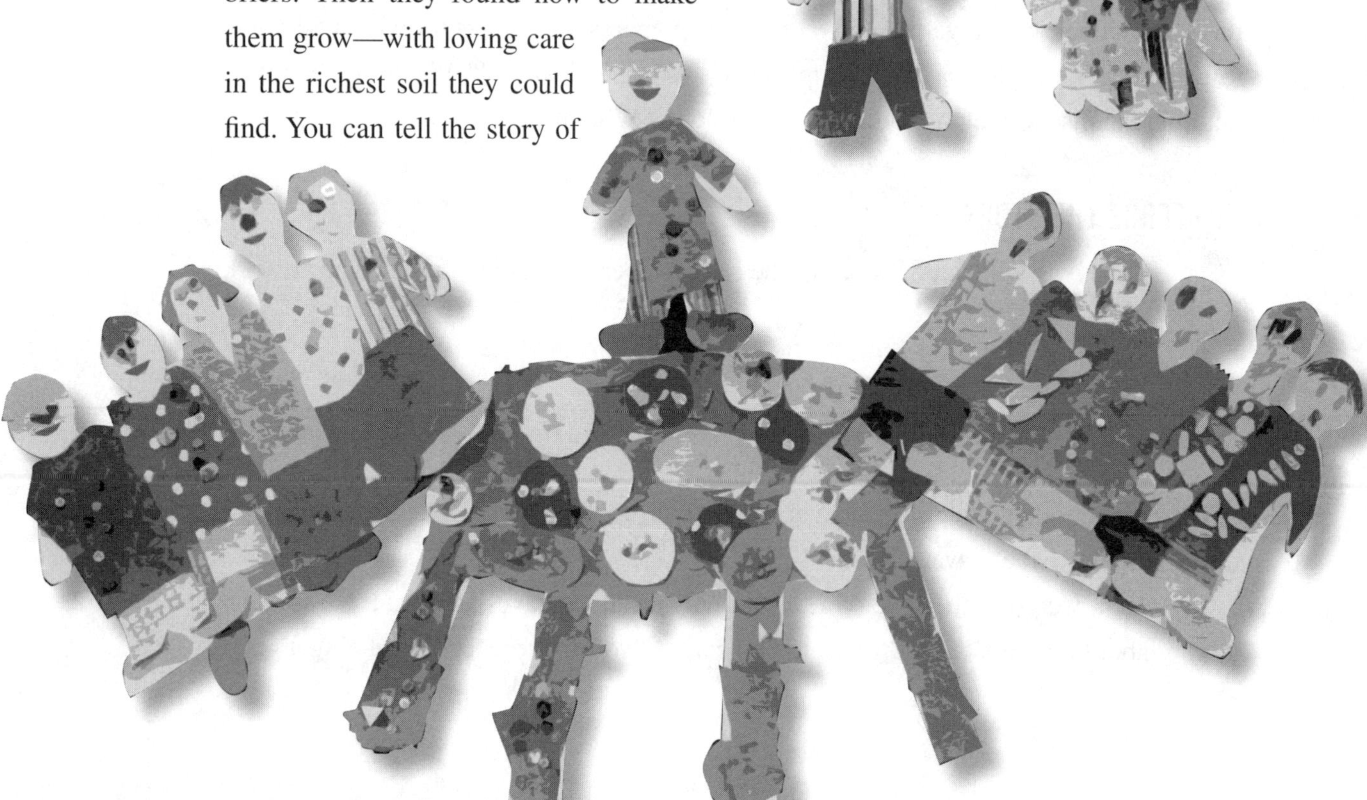

the little mustard seed that grew and grew and grew. You can tell the story of the Good Samaritan who stopped for the one in need when everyone else passed by. They are your stories now, and you should tell them and more."

Jesus continued, "And when you tell these stories, I am with you. When you watch a butterfly flutter by on a spring breeze, or the sun set over the sea, or feel the wind blow through your hair, I am there. When you help a friend or hug someone who is feeling lonesome, I am with you. When you sing with all your heart, when you laugh and laugh and laugh with joy, I am there. When you are sad; when you are happy, I am with you. My love will always be with you."

And Jesus died, but his love lives on. His stories and the way he led his life guides us all in making choices about who we want to be.

AFTER THE STORY

And that is the story of the Last Supper and part of the Easter Story. Here we try to take care of each other and share our happiness and our times of sadness. Let's all sing, "Love Begins with Giving" on page 240-241.

STORY-TELLING TIPS

- When the listener is reminded of the stories they have heard in other chapels, you can expand or contract the details from those stories according to how long ago they heard them. You can have one of the disciples ask Jesus to retell one of the stories if you want to emphasize one aspect or the children would like to hear a story again.
- For the details of when Jesus is present in one's life, you can add specifics from your area—places of beauty or circumstances where children might have an opportunity to help someone.
- You might have Jesus sing the "I Want to Thank You" refrain to the disciples when they first gather.

ART NEEDS

- Jesus
- The disciples
- A big table full of food

STORY SKELETON

- Jesus and disciples have been traveling doing their work, sometimes together and at other times separately.
- It is time for the Passover celebration.
- Jesus calls all the disciples together.
- They sit around a large table where they will eat.
- Jesus breaks the bread.
- Jesus tells disciples this is their last supper together.
- They ask why.
- He says that soon he will die.
- They ask why.
- He says there are people who don't like what he is doing.
- Disciples ask about what they will do without Jesus.
- He tells them to keep telling the stories.
- He reminds them of the stories.
- He then tells them how he will always be with them.
- He will be with them when they do something kind, or share or when they are sad or happy, or when they see wondrous sights or hear amazing sounds.
- Jesus says he will always be with them.

part 5

STORIES OF THE VALUE OF ALL LIVING THINGS

chapter 22

THE PARABLE OF THE LOST SHEEP
LUKE 15:3-7

A Story about the Value of Each Individual

Sing-along "Everything Counts" (p. 239)

Often a young child feels lost at school with so many other children around, especially after a summer break. Because of this we generally share this story early in the fall to let all the children know that they are in good care, and that each of them is noticed.

BEFORE THE STORY

Today we are sharing another story from the Bible, but it's from a different part of the Bible than the last two chapel stories (often The Creation Story and The Garden of Eden). They were from the Old Testament. This is a story that Jesus told and is found in the New Testament. The artwork is by _______ .

THE STORY

Optional beginning

(Depending on when in the year you are sharing the story, you may choose to introduce Jesus who told the story or just tell the parable and begin with the song "Sleep, Sheep, Sleep.")

Wherever Jesus went, he told stories, sometimes called parables. People loved to hear these parables and gathered wherever he was. The stories Jesus told were so rich, full of meaning. Jesus used these stories to help people think about his message of love and sharing and caring for each other. One day he told a story of a shepherd with a whole flock of sheep and one little sheep that got lost. The parable goes like this:

♫ **I have counted one, two, three,**
All the way to one hundred sheep.
Now it's time to go to sleep.
Sleep, sheep, sleep.

There once was a shepherd. His job was to take care of the sheep. The flock of sheep the shepherd took care of was big. In fact, there were one hundred sheep. Every morning the shepherd sent the sheep out into the fields where they played and ran and jumped in the grass, drank from the stream, and ate grass in the pastures on the hill-sides. While the sheep played and ate, the shepherd kept watch over them walking from field to field making sure they were safe.

At the end of the day, he gathered the sheep together. How did they know it was time? He called them by playing his flute. When the sheep heard his tune, they answered, "Baa," and came running across the fields. Once they were all together at his feet, he counted them: 1, 2, 3, 4, 5, 6, 7, 8, 9, 10, 11, and on and on until he got to the last few—98, 99, 100. Then he sang a lullaby.

♫ **I have counted one, two, three,**
All the way to one hundred sheep.
Now it's time to go to sleep.
Sleep, sheep, sleep.

And that is how it went every day. In the morning the shepherd sent the sheep out to play. Then he walked across the fields making sure they were safe. At the end of the day, he played his flute to call the sheep, listened for their "baa," gathered them together, and counted them again. 1, 2, 3, 4, 5, 6, 7, 8, 9, 10, 11, and on and on until he got to the last few—98, 99, 100. Then he sang the lullaby.

♫ **I have counted one, two three,**
All the way to one hundred sheep.
Now it's time to go to sleep.
Sleep, sheep, sleep.

But one day it was different. Well, it started out the same. He sent the sheep out to play, as usual. He walked across the fields watching the sheep eating, and drinking from the stream, and playing in the tall grass. But on this day, he was thinking about the evening when the sheep were all asleep. You see, that evening there was to be a festival in the village, and he was looking forward to going there with his friends. The festival always offered good food, lively music, and festive dancing.

As the sun began to set, a few of the shepherd's friends came up the hill to ask him to join them for the festival. He replied, "I'll be ready in a moment. I just have to gather the sheep." So he played his flute. When they heard his tune, the sheep "baa-ed" and gathered around the shepherd. He counted them: 1, 2, 3, 4, 5, 6, 7, 8, 9, 10, 11, and on and on until he got to the last few—98, 99, —.

The shepherd was amazed! He said, "Wait a minute, I must have made a mistake. I've got to count again." One of his friends called, "Come on! Let's go!" The shepherd replied, "Just a second. I must have miscounted the sheep. I just have to count again." So he counted again: 1, 2, 3, 4, 5, 6, 7, 8, 9, 10, 11, and on and on until he got to the last few—98, 99, —. "Oh no!" said the shepherd, "one of my sheep is missing." He looked over the sheep, and because he was a very good shepherd, he knew every sheep, and soon he knew which sheep was missing. It was one of the smallest ones.

The shepherd's friends called to him again, "Let's go! It's getting late. The festival has already begun," The shepherd answered, "But one of my sheep is missing." "How many sheep do you have?" they asked. "One hundred," replied the shepherd. The friends smiled and said, "You have ninety-nine sheep and you're worried about just one? One sheep doesn't matter that much. Come on." Then one of the friends added, "Anyway, it will probably show up tomorrow." The shepherd shook his head, "I can't take that chance. I need to know that every single sheep is here with me safe before I can do anything. Friends, you go ahead to the festival. I'll see you after *all* my sheep are together again." So the friends went down the hill toward the village festival while the shepherd headed in the other direction looking for the lost sheep.

He thought, "Maybe she's down by the stream!" But when he arrived down near the water, he didn't see her. He noticed a big tree. "Maybe she's behind the tree," he exclaimed. So he pulled out his flute and played the tune he always played to gather the sheep. He played and listened. There was no response—no "baa!" He looked behind the tree. No lost sheep. Then he spied a big bush. "Maybe she's behind the bush." He played the tune again and listened. No "baa"—no sheep. Then he saw a big rock. He thought, "Maybe my little sheep is there!" So he played his flute again and listened. This time he heard a small call. "Baa!" and the little lost sheep ran out from behind the rock. The shepherd picked up the little sheep and carried it back to the flock.

He gathered his flock together and counted them all just to be sure: 1, 2, 3, 4, 5, 6, 7, 8, 9, 10, 11, and on and on until he got to the last few—98, 99, 100! All together again, safe and sound! The shepherd smiled and sang to his sheep

♫ **I have counted one, two, three,**
All the way to one hundred sheep.
Now it's time to go to sleep.
Sleep, sheep, sleep.

Optional ending

You may wish to end with the song above. Or like this

The story was over. Jesus looked around at all the people. Some were looking back at him. Others had their eyes closed, allowing his words to play in their minds. Still others were watching the clouds move across the sky as they thought about the story. One person exclaimed, "Everyone counts!" Jesus smiled and nodded.

AFTER THE STORY

And here at school we know that each and every one is very important. Now we'll sing "Everything Counts."

STORY-TELLING TIPS

- If you or one of your colleagues is a musician, any time the shepherd calls his sheep, the first line of the "Sleep, Sheep, Sleep" melody can be played on a flute or a recorder. Likewise, when the shepherd looks for the little sheep, this same melody is played to call the lost one.
- When calling the sheep, play the melody, pause, cup your hand around one ear to listen, and then "baa" for the sheep's reply. Use this same routine when looking for the lost sheep, and the children will understand that they

are listening for the lost sheep's call. When it does reply from behind the rock, the "baa" will delight the children.

- This same strategy can be used without a musician by describing the playing of the instrument—i.e., "He played his flute and then listened." (Pause) "Baa."
- For this story you might want to pre-set the artwork tree, bush, and rock with the lost sheep behind it. This will make the finding of the sheep more of a surprise later. You can then introduce the artwork of the shepherd and the flock of sheep as you tell the story.

ART NEEDS

- Shepherd
- Lots of sheep
- One little sheep
- Rock to hide behind (Little sheep should be able to fit behind rock unseen.)
- Bush to hide behind
- Tree to hide behind

STORY SKELETON

- Jesus told parables

Sleep, Sheep, Sleep

(Parable of the Lost Sheep)

Bill Gordh

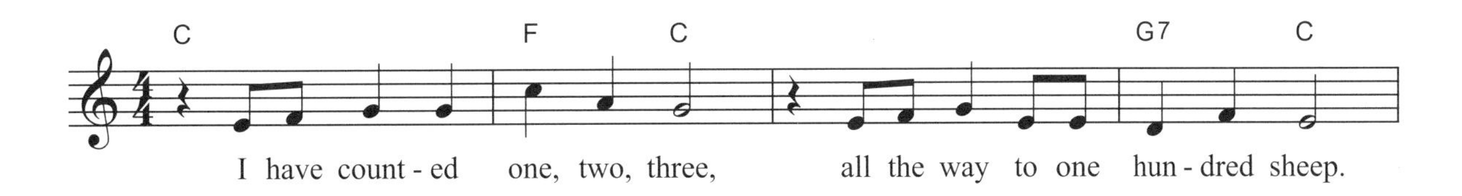

- Shepherd has one hundred sheep.
- Each day he sends them into the fields.
- He watches over them.
- At the end of the day he calls his sheep with a melody on his flute.
- He counts all one hundred sheep.
- He sings a lullaby to sheep.

♫

- Repeat the sequence of sheep in field, the calling and counting of the sheep, and the lullaby.
- Then one day, the shepherd calls the sheep.
- He counts the sheep. One to 98, 99,—.
- He counts the sheep again. One to 98, 99,—.
- One sheep is missing!
- His friends come to urge him to join them for a village celebration.
- He says, “No.”
- Friends say, “One sheep doesn’t make a difference.”
- Shepherd says, “Each sheep is important.”
- He goes to look for the lost sheep.
- He plays his flute near a tree and listens.
- No “baa” from the lost sheep.
- He plays his flute near a bush and listens.
- No “baa” from the lost sheep.
- He plays his flute near a rock and listens.
- “Baa” from the lost sheep.
- He carries the lost sheep back to the others.
- He counts the sheep. One to 98, 99, 100.
- He sings the lullaby.

♫

chapter 23

JESUS AND ALL THE CHILDREN
LUKE 18:15-17

A Story about the Importance of Children

Sing Along "Everything Counts" (p. 239)

Any story with children as characters has immediate appeal to young listeners. Children often feel excluded from important events and discussions in their family life and in the world in general. They have all experienced being pushed aside. The story of Jesus calling for the children to be near and for him to announce to all their importance is a very empowering listening experience.

BEFORE THE STORY

Today we will be sharing another story from the Bible. It is about Jesus on his travels and the children that wanted to hear him speak.

THE STORY

Jesus and his disciples traveled from town to town, village to village sharing his stories of love and caring. One day they stopped just outside a village. It was a lovely place, and Jesus felt that people would enjoy being there with him. So Jesus sat down beneath a huge oak with big spreading branches. He sat down to wait for the people from the village.

In the village everyone had been talking about Jesus for days. They had heard some travelers talking about the wonderful stories Jesus told. The children were excited as well. All the children were talking about Jesus coming to their village. All the children were making their plans to meet Jesus. They all wanted to hear his stories.

When word spread that Jesus was sitting under the oak just outside of town, all the work stopped. Farmers set aside their plows, shepherds left the fields, cooks stopped cooking, sweepers ceased sweeping, and all the children stopped playing. They all started down the road to the place where Jesus waited. There were women and men, grandmothers and grandfathers, and all the children in the village. The children were talking and jumping and laughing. They were excited. Soon they would see the man they had heard so much about. Soon they would hear his stories of love and kindness.

But as they got closer, the children saw some men blocking the way! They were men they had never seen before. The men had very serious looks on their faces. They were stopping the families before they could see Jesus! What were they saying?

"We're sorry," said these men who were the disciples, "but you must send your children home! Jesus is far too busy to talk to children. The grown-ups may come ahead, but all the children must go back home! Now!!"

The children could not believe it. Not see Jesus! Not hear his stories! They turned sadly around and started back into the village. "Don't worry, children. We'll tell you everything that Jesus says," called out a couple of the parents.

Jesus looked up as the disciples came closer with a group of grown-ups from the village. They waited for him to speak, but he didn't say a word. Jesus looked around. Finally he asked the disciples, "Where are all the children?" The disciples quickly replied, "Don't worry Jesus. The children won't bother you. We sent them home!"

Jesus looked at his disciples in amazement. Then he spoke, "You sent them home? The children!? You sent them home!?"

"Yes," said the disciples, "We told them you were too busy to see them. Now you can talk to the grown-ups."

Jesus shook his head. "My friends," he said. "Thank you for what you are trying to do, but you have it all mixed up."

♫ **And Jesus said,**
"Go tell all the children,
'Come unto me, come unto me, come unto me.'
Go tell all the children,
'Come unto me.
Each is just as special as anyone can be.'"

The disciples realized their terrible mistake. They went running, but some of the mothers and fathers had heard what Jesus said, and they were way ahead of the disciples. When the parents came running in, the children looked up and asked, "What did Jesus say?" The parents answered,

♫ **Well, Jesus said,**
" Go tell all the children,
'Come unto me, come unto me, come unto me.'
Go tell all the children,
'Come unto me.
Each is just as special as anyone can be.'"

The children barely heard the end of the song, for they were running up the road to Jesus. When they arrived, the grown-ups moved aside, and the children came and sat with Jesus. Some sat on his lap, others at his feet, all so very close. He told the children stories—stories of sharing, stories of caring, and stories of how the love of God goes on and on and on.

AFTER THE STORY

And we tell this story here at ________ because "all the children" are so important to us. Now let's sing "Everything Counts."

STORY-TELLING TIPS

- You may notice that the phrase "all the children" is used frequently in the text. It is offered casually so that the listeners hear the phrase, and when it becomes central to the story, it enhances its meaning. Therefore you don't need to emphasize the phrase until it is used in the refrain.
- If you speak the refrain instead of singing it, you might have a couple of colleagues join you when the parents repeat to the children what Jesus said.

ART NEEDS

- Jesus
- Some disciples
- Children
- Some parents
- A big tree

STORY SKELETON

- Jesus and the disciples continued their travels, sharing stories and teaching.
- They came to a village.
- Jesus noticed a beautiful tree.
- He told the disciples he would sit beneath the tree and talk with people.
- Word spread through the village that Jesus was under the tree.
- Everyone came – old and young alike.
- The children were excited and skipping and talking.
- The disciples hurried down the road to quiet things down.
- They sent the children home.
- They said Jesus only had time for grown-ups.
- The children sadly went home.
- The grown-ups went and stood near Jesus to listen.
- Jesus waited.
- Jesus asked where everyone was.
- The disciples explained that they had sent the children home.

Come unto Me

(Jesus and Children)

Bill Gordh

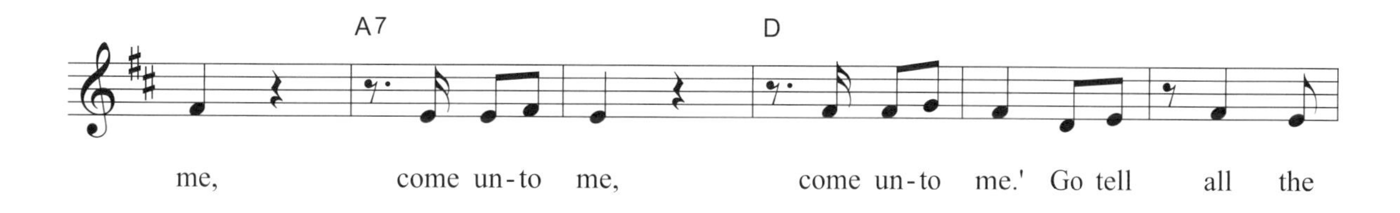

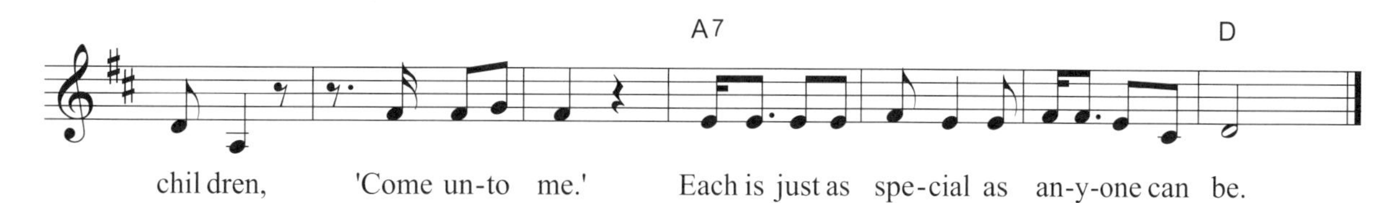

- The parents were ahead of the disciples and tell the children

♫

- The children came running and gathered around Jesus.
- Jesus told story after story about working together and being good neighbors and how the love of God goes on and on and on.

chapter 24

THE PARABLE OF THE SOWERS
MARK 4:2-8

A Story of Taking Care

Sing-along "In My Garden" (p. 244-245)

In the Bible Jesus tells the story of a sower, sowing his seeds in different places. Here, the sower has been turned into two, a boy and a girl. They visit a farmer who offers them seeds to plant. The telling provides children a more direct connection to the story.

BEFORE THE STORY

Last week we heard the story about Jesus and the crowd of five thousand and a girl who shared her lunch. Today's story is one Jesus told about a farmer and two children. The artwork is by _______ .

THE STORY

After Jesus found his helpers or "disciples," he began his work. They traveled from town to town talking to people about the love of God, about sharing and caring, working together and being good friends and neighbors. Sometimes Jesus just talked and sometimes Jesus told stories. The stories are called parables, and this is one of them. It is called "The Parable of the Sowers," and a sower is someone who plants seeds.

Once there was a farmer, and one day she called in two of her children friends—a sister and brother. She held out a handful of seeds and suggested that they could sow the seeds. The farmer told the children that it was important to plant the seeds carefully.

♫ **Oh sow your seeds with special care.**
They will not grow just anywhere.
They need love; give them their share,
And you'll see them growin'
With seeds to spare.

So the boy took some seeds, and he started walking and thinking about where to sow them. Well, he decided to just drop them along the path. He got to the end of the path and turned to look at what he had done. Just then some crows flew over his head. "Caw – Caw!" they cried and swooped down. The boy watched as the crows ate up the seeds he had just dropped along the path. He shook his head. Dropping them along the path was not a good way to help them grow. He walked back and told them what happened with his seeds.

♫ **There was a boy who took his seeds**
And dropped them on the path he walked.
Some crows flew by, and when they did spy
Those seeds he let fly, they ate fine,
And they did squawk. Caw Caw!
Oh, sow your seeds with special care.
They will not grow just anywhere.
They need love; give them their share,
And you'll see them growing,
With seeds to spare.

Now it was the girl's turn. She took some seeds from the farmer and walked down the path. She knew this was not a good spot to sow her seeds so she kept walking. She came to some rocky ground, stopped, and threw her seeds there. The soil was hard and rocks covered the hard earth. Well, some of the seeds began to root, but not for long. The wind began to blow and blew away the seeds. She watched the seeds drift off in the wind. She shook her head. The rocky ground was not a good place for growing new plants. She sadly walked back and told them what happened.

♫ **There was a girl who took her seeds**
And sowed them on the rocky ground.
At first they grew, but when the wind blew
Those seeds that she threw, they flew
And could not be found.

Oh, sow your seeds with special care.
They will not grow just anywhere.
They need love; give them their share,
And you'll see them growing,
With seeds to spare.

So the brother and sister took some more seeds from the farmer's outstretched hand. They walked down the path, and they were careful not to drop any there. They walked right by the rocky ground; they were careful not to drop any there either. Then they came to a brier patch, where thick, thorny bushes were growing. They decided to give that spot a try and threw their seeds into the patch. Well, the briers kept away the sun and the rain, so the seeds could not grow. The sister and brother looked at each other and shook their heads. The briar patch was not a good place to sow their seeds.

♫ **They took their seeds and walked along**
And dropped some in a briar patch.
The briars choked their little throats,
And the seeds lost all hope; there they go
And that is that.
Oh, sow your seeds with special care.
They will not grow just anywhere.
They need love; give them their share,
And you'll see them growing,
With seeds to spare.

The brother and sister went back to the farmer. The farmer asked them how it was going. The boy answered first, "Well, I sowed some seeds along the path, but the crows ate them." The sister added, "Then I threw some seeds on the rocky ground, and the wind blew them away." Then they both said, "Then the last seeds you gave us, we threw in a briar patch but the briars kept away the sun and rain, so nothing grew. We don't have any seeds left. Can we have some more?"

The farmer opened her hand. There were just a few seeds left. "These are all the seeds that are left, but you can take them." The sister and brother took the seeds, thanked the farmer, and walked along. They thought about what the farmer had told them, about taking care of the seeds, and how seeds won't grow just anywhere. Seeds need loving care. So they walked along the path, past the rocky ground, past the briar patch, and on until they found a special place. It was a spot where the earth was dark and rich. It was a place where the sun would shine and rain could fall. They dug in the dirt and planted the last seeds with great care. They patted down the dirt and watered the spot. They watched as the sun shown down and as the rain fell. They watched as the plants began to grow. They weeded around the new plants and watered them when the rain did not fall. The plants kept growing. They grew and grew and grew and when the plants were big, those plants sowed their own seeds, and those seeds took root. Then new plants grew and those plants had more seeds, and those seeds grew more plants, and on and on and soon the sister and brother had a whole field full of beautiful plants.

They ran to the farmer's house. The farmer saw them coming and called out, "I have not seen you two for a long time. Where have you been?" They ran up onto the porch and answered together, "We've been taking care! Come!" The sister took the farmer's hand, and the brother took the other, and they led her to the top of a hill. They told her to close her eyes and then—"Take a look!" they cried out. The farmer opened her eyes and looked down across the golden fields. "Wow!" she exclaimed.

They only had a few seeds left.

♫ **They wondered where they'd ever grow.**
They dropped the seeds in the earth so deep;
Gave them everything they need. What did they reap?
Fields of gold.
They dropped the seeds in the earth so deep
Gave them everything they need. What did they reap?
Fields of gold.

And the story was over. People looked at Jesus and told him that they loved the tale. But one person said, "Jesus, that is a great story, but we are not farmers. So why did you tell us that tale?" And Jesus said, "We are all farmers, but the seeds we sow are different. The seeds we sow are the seeds of love and friendship. When we take special care of those seeds, the friendships grow and become stronger, and the friends make other friends, and those friendships grow, and the love and friendship grow and grow and grow. That is the way the love of God works."

And that is the story of "The Sowers."

AFTER THE STORY

This story reminds us how important it is to take care of our friends and family and everyone we love. And that with care friendships will grow and grow and grow just like the plants in a garden. Now we'll sing "In My Garden."

STORY-TELLING TIPS

- The story works fine without including the song. If you do not use the song, you might expand a bit on the details of each sowing. You can just speak the chorus when the farmer first advises the two children.
- When you tell what a sower is, you may want to add that it is not "sewing" and demonstrate with your hands the physical actions of the two terms. This will make it clearer than just word definitions.
- If you use the song, you might have a guest singer sing the verses and then join in on the chorus. Then the children get to hear the story told as a narrative and as a song. Also, after hearing the story and song together, the song can be used as a sing-along for other chapel times.
- The farmer is presented as a woman.

ART NEEDS

- Farmer
- Boy
- Girl
- Seeds
- Path (optional)
- Rocky ground (optional)
- Briar patch (optional)
- Fields of Gold (grain field) (optional)

STORY SKELETON

- Boy and girl visit farmer.
- She tells them they can plant seeds today.
- She tells them to plant the seeds with care.

♫ (chorus from song below)

- The boy goes first.
- He takes some seeds and drops them along the path he's walking.
- At the end of the path he turns around to see what he has done.
- Crows fly down and eat the seeds.
- The boy goes back and tells them what happened.

Sow Your Seeds

(The Parable of the Sower)

Bill Gordh

- The girl takes some seeds and walks down the path.
- At the end of the path, she throws her seeds on the rocky ground.
- The seeds begin to sprout, but when the wind starts up, the seedlings blow away.
- The girl goes back and tells them what happened.

♫

- The boy and girl take some seeds.

- They walk down the path, past the rocky ground, and throw the seeds into the briars.
- The briars keep out the sun and the plants cannot grow.

♫

- They go back.
- They take the last few seeds the farmer offers.
- They walk down the path, past the rocky ground, and past the briar patch.
- They find a place where the earth is rich, where the sun can shine and the rain can fall.
- They carefully dig holes and plant the last few seeds.
- They return to weed the plants and to water them when it doesn't rain.
- The plants grow and drop seeds, and the seeds grow more plants and then more seeds and on and on and on.
- The children run back to the farmer and bring her back with them.
- They show her the field of plants that are still growing.

♫

- If we take care of our friendships, they will grow and grow.

chapter 25

THE PARABLE OF THE MUSTARD SEED
MATTHEW 13:31-32

A Story about the Importance of All, Regardless of Size

Sing-along "Everything Counts" (p. 239)

A story in the Bible that is as small as a mustard seed grows in the children's chapel as a brother and sister learn about the importance of even the smallest seed. We generally use this parable at the end of the school year to offer a story in which the children can reflect on how their friendships have grown over the year.

BEFORE THE STORY

Today our story is from the Bible. It's a story that Jesus told about a little seed. The artwork today is by _________ .

THE STORY

And Jesus told this story

One day the sister and brother went back to see the farmer. They had not seen her for quite a while and were excited. They ran up onto her porch. She was happy to see them as well. The farmer smiled. "Great to see you," she said, "I have a new story for you." "What's it about?" asked the two at the same time.

"It's about seeds," she replied. "We've heard that story already," said the children. "You have?" asked the farmer. "Yes," said the brother. "Remember, you gave us the seeds, and I took a handful and dropped them along the pathway. They didn't grow there; the crows ate them." "Then," added the sister, "I took some seeds and threw them on the rocky ground. They didn't grow there either; the wind blew them away." Sister and brother added, "Then we threw a bunch of seeds in the briars. They didn't grow there either." The farmer asked them, "What did you discover then?" "Well," they said, "After that we planted the rest of the seeds very carefully in deep dark soil. Then we weeded them and made sure they got plenty of sun and water. Then they grew beautifully! See, we already know that story."

"Well," said the farmer, "You certainly know that story, and because you know how to make things grow, it's time for another story about seeds." She held out her hand and opened it. "Take a look!"

Sister and brother looked in the farmer's hand. They saw a great big seed. They grabbed the great big seed. "Can we plant it?" they asked. "Sure," replied the farmer, and watched them as they ran down the hill and across the field. They stopped at the edge of their new garden. There they dug a deep hole in the rich dark soil and dropped the seed in. They covered it over and pulled out all the weeds nearby. It was a perfect place for sun and rain. Then they ran back to the farmer.

"The great big seed is planted. What's next?" The farmer held out her hand again. "Take a look!" she said. This time they saw a medium-sized seed. "This looks like a good one too!" exclaimed the sister. "Can we plant it?" asked the brother. "Sure," replied the farmer, and she watched the two as they ran down the hill and across the field. They ran to the garden and once again carefully planted it, this time in the middle. Then they ran back to the farmer. "What's next?" they asked. The farmer held out her hand again. "Take a look!" she said to the sister and brother. The children looked in her hand. They looked at the farmer. "Are you trying to trick us?" they asked. "There's nothing in your hand." The farmer smiled, "Look again," she responded.

The children peered into her hand and after a while noticed a tiny, tiny seed in one of the creases. "That is the tiniest seed we've ever seen. I don't know if it's even worth planting," said the children. "It's a mustard seed," said the farmer, "and you can choose to plant it or not. It's up to you." The sister and brother looked at each other and nodded. "We're going to plant it too!" they announced.

They took the tiny mustard seed and ran down the hill and across the field. When they got to the garden, they walked to the far side and planted it just as carefully as they had the bigger seeds. They took care of all their seeds and watered the garden when there was not enough rain.

One day the farmer heard a knock on her door. "Come with us!" cried the children, "Come with us!" The farmer followed the excited children down the hill and across the field. As they neared the garden, they stopped and asked the farmer to close her eyes. She did, and the sister and brother held her hands as they walked to the edge of the garden. Then they sang out.

♫ **Take a look, take a look!**
Take a look
And see what we have done.
Take a look, take a look!
Take a look
How the great big seed has grown!

And there stood a beautiful big plant. "Good job," exclaimed the farmer, "That is a big beautiful healthy plant. Did it grow from the big seed?" "Right!" exclaimed the children. "Is there more?" asked the farmer. "Yes! Come on," they replied. As they neared the middle of the garden, once again they asked the farmer to close her eyes and carefully led her along. Then they sang,

♫ **Take a look, take a look!**
Take a look
And see what we have done.
Take a look, take a look!
Take a look
How the middle-sized seed has grown!

And there was another beautiful plant, not as big as the first but still lovely. "This grew from the medium seed," said the children. "Nice work!" said the farmer. "How about that tiny, tiny mustard seed?" The children smiled, "Come. Close your eyes. We'll lead you." They led the farmer across the garden. When they got to the far end of the garden, they sang out,

♫ **Take a look, take a look!**
Take a look
And see what we have done.
Take a look, take a look!
Take a look
How the little bitty seed has grown!

The farmer opened her eyes and looked where the children were pointing. There stood the largest plant in the garden. "Wow!" said the farmer, "It grew from the tiniest seed."

"That's right," said the children, "And we nearly didn't plant it at all."

And Jesus had finished his story. The people listening said, "That was a neat story but we are not farmers. So why did you tell it to *us*?" Jesus looked at the people gathered. He smiled, "That little mustard seed is like the beginnings of love and friendship. At first it seems like not much at all, but with care and time it grows into a love that is as big as the world!"

AFTER THE STORY

Here at ________ we watch as the little seeds of friendship grow and grow and grow. Now we'll sing "Everything Counts."

STORY-TELLING TIPS

- If you have not told the story of "The Sower," you can skip the part in the story when the children recount that story and go directly to planting the three seeds.
- The farmer closing her eyes is a fun addition, and often children will close their eyes like the farmer. Then you put up the artwork each time as the farmer (and the children listeners) opens her eyes. With the mustard seed, if

they haven't already, ask the children to close their eyes too.

- If the children have made the artwork of the three plants, you can have the farmer comment on the beauty of each plant, specifically calling attention to aesthetic choices the children have made.
- I like to finish this story sometimes with Jesus asking his listeners why they think he told the story. I then describe how one of the children offers the comment that Jesus makes in the text. This suggests that children can think about the stories themselves and come to their own conclusions rather than asking a grown-up to supply the answer.

ART NEEDS

- Brother and sister
- Farmer
- Little tiny, tiny, tiny, tiny, tiny, tiny, tiny seed
- Medium seed
- Large seed
- Medium-sized plant
- Big plant
- Huge plant

STORY SKELETON

- Sister and brother visit farmer.
- She says she has a new story about seeds.
- They say they know it.
- Brother and sister talk about the tale of the sowers.
- Brother describes how he dropped seeds along the path and the crows ate them.
- Sister describes how she sowed seeds on the rocky ground and the wind blew them away.
- They both describe how the briars choked the next seed plantings.
- They then tell how the seeds grew when treated with care.
- Farmer says it is a new story.
- She holds out her hand. "Take a look!"
- They take a big seed from her hand.

- They plant the big seed and return.
- She holds out her hand. "Take a look!"
- They take a medium-sized seed from her hand.
- They plant the seed and return.
- She holds out her hand. "Take a look!"
- They don't see anything.
- Farmer holds out her hand again. "Take a look!"
- At first they see nothing.
- They see a little tiny seed.
- They take the seed from her hand, but think it might be too small to plant.
- She lets them decide whether to plant it.
- They plant it at the far side of garden.
- They weed and water. Plants grow.
- They come back to the farmer.
- They bring her to the garden.
- They ask her to close her eyes.

Take a Look!

(Parable of the Mustard Seed)

Bill Gordh

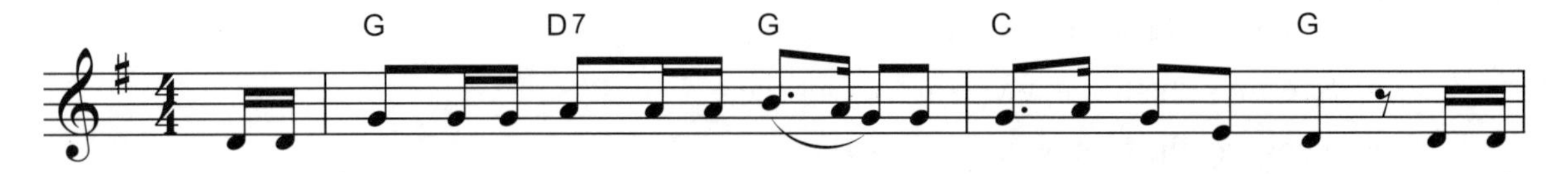

- She looks. Big seed—big green plant.
- She admires the plant.
- They walk her to the middle of the garden.
- They ask her to close her eyes.

♫

- She looks. Middle-sized seed—middle-sized green plant.
- She admires the plant.
- They walk her to the end of the garden.
- They ask her to close her eyes.

♫

- She looks. Little tiny seed—HUGE green plant.
- Farmer expresses her delight.
- The story is over.
- People ask Jesus why he told the story.
- Love and friendship start out as little tiny seeds, almost nothing at all.
- With care, the friendships grow bigger and bigger and bigger.

part 6

STORIES OF GIVING AND FORGIVING

chapter 26

TWO LITTLE FISH AND FIVE LOAVES OF BREAD

MATTHEW 14:13-18; JOHN 6:1-15

A Story about Generosity

Sing-along "Love Begins with Giving" (p. 240-241)

The story of Jesus feeding five thousand people with just a small amount of food is often told to demonstrate the miraculous powers of Jesus. The telling here is centered on the generosity of the little girl who offers to share her lunch.

BEFORE THE STORY

This is a story from the Bible about Jesus, a little girl, and more than five thousand hungry people. The artwork is by _______ .

THE STORY

Jesus kept traveling, traveling and telling stories, traveling and talking to new friends. The more he traveled, the more people heard the healing words that he spoke. The more he spoke, the more people talked of the man named Jesus, the man who told the wondrous stories of love and forgiveness, of sharing and caring and the endless love of God. At each place Jesus stopped, the number of people ready to hear his words grew and grew.

On the day of this story, the Bible says there were more than five thousand people gathered to listen to Jesus. There were girls and boys, men and women, grandmothers and grandfathers, and of course the disciples were there. They all wanted to hear the stories Jesus had to tell. And that is what Jesus did. He told stories and spoke of the love of God. He told the story of the farmer and sowing seeds with care. He told the story of the tiny mustard seed, and how it grew. Jesus told the story of the shepherd and the lost sheep and the tale of the Good Samaritan. The morning went by, and it was time for lunch. Everyone was hungry but no one wanted to leave. No one wanted to miss even one word that Jesus might speak. There was rumbling, but it wasn't thunder; it wasn't upset people. The rumbling was coming from hungry tummies. The crowd of people really needed lunch. The disciples scratched their heads. They didn't know what to do!

Just then, Jesus heard a voice from the crowd. The voice said, "I'll share my lunch!" He looked to see who was speaking. There near the front of the seated crowd was a little girl with a basket in her lap. Jesus smiled. He asked the girl, "What do you have?" and she replied, "Let me see. I have one, two—two little fish and one, two, three, four, five—five loaves of bread." She looked at Jesus and announced, "I have two little fish and five loaves of bread." Jesus smiled. The disciples laughed and asked the girl, "What?" And she said again, "Two little fish and five loaves of bread."

Jesus looked at his disciples and then out across the crowd of five thousand. He gazed again at the girl with her lunch basket. He got an idea and asked the disciples to bring him the basket. The little girl handed the disciples her basket, and they brought it to Jesus. Jesus began breaking the bread and handing the pieces to the disciples to give out. Each disciple went out into the crowd, passed out some bread and came back. Jesus handed out more bread. Out they went again and again with more bread. The same thing happened with the fish. Over and over and over until every one of those five thousand people was eating bread and fish!

Then Jesus asked the disciples to gather up any uneaten portions, as no food should be wasted. Soon they were back with twelve baskets of leftovers, enough bread and fish to take to the next village. Jesus thanked the girl when he handed her basket back to her. Then Jesus spoke once again to the crowd, "I want to thank this young girl for sharing her lunch. There is nothing greater than a generous heart." Everyone looked at the smiling, slightly embarrassed girl. The disciples turned their attention back to Jesus. Jesus had just fed five thousand people with two little fish and five loaves of bread! They were amazed. "Why are you surprised?" asked Jesus, "This little girl just shared all the lunch she had, and you know how love grows."

And that is the story of one generous girl who gave from her heart and helped feed a crowd with only two little fish and five loaves of bread.

AFTER THE STORY

And just like this story of the generous girl whose gift grew and grew and grew, here at _____________, love begins with a little generosity and keeps growing and growing and growing. Now we'll sing "Love Begins with Giving."

STORY-TELLING TIPS

- You might want to tell the story with a sister and brother, instead of just a girl. Then it shows a boy and girl being generous. On the other hand, with so many stories featuring all or mostly men, having the one girl may be a nice change of pace.
- When telling of stories that Jesus told to the crowd, name stories that your listeners have heard and perhaps one or two that they will hear. This makes them feel comfortable and like one of the children listening to Jesus in the story. When you come to one of the new stories later in the year, the children will have already heard about it and be excited to hear the whole tale.
- There's a wonderful song version of this story written by Sister Rosetta Tharpe, the gospel singer and songwriter, that you might want to play and or sing for/with the children.

ART NEEDS

- Jesus
- Crowd (optional)
- Disciples—three or four (optional)
- Basket (optional)
- Two little fish
- Five loaves of bread
- Girl

STORY SKELETON

- Jesus and disciples travel town to town.
- More and more people want to hear the stories.
- There are five thousand people.
- Jesus shares his stories of God's love, being good neighbors, sharing, caring and working together.
- It gets to be lunchtime.
- Everyone is hungry, but no one wants to leave.
- A girl offers her basket of food.
- She has two little fish and five loaves of bread.
- The disciples laugh.
- Jesus says not to laugh, but bring the food to him.
- He begins to break the bread and fish and pass it to the disciples to distribute.
- They go out and come back.
- Jesus continues giving them more bread and fish.
- The whole crowd is fed.
- There are leftovers!
- It all began with the generosity of a girl willing to share her lunch.

chapter 27

THE THREE KINGS AND THE YOUNG GIRL

MATTHEW 2:1-12

A Story about Giving

Sing-along "Love Begins with Giving" (p. 240-241)

Children love to hear about the royal wise men that travel from afar following the star with exotic gifts for the little baby Jesus. In the context of a children's chapel, it is important that this exoticism doesn't distract the young listener from the true value of a gift. With this in mind, as in Menotti's opera *Amahl and the Night Visitors* and the Christmas song "The Little Drummer Boy," we add a character that journeys with the three kings to see the baby.

BEFORE THE STORY

Today's story is about three kings and a new addition to an old tale, a little girl who joins them to go and see the baby Jesus. The artwork is by _________.

THE STORY

At the time of the birth of Jesus there were three kings living far to the east. The kings were wise men who studied the stars. One night they saw the brightest star that they had ever seen. They came together to talk about this amazing sight. They knew that the star was announcing a very special event, and they saw that it was shining down on a place very far away. "A prince is born!" exclaimed one of the kings. "We must go see him now and pay our respects," added the second king, "for he will be a great leader when he becomes a man." The third king said, "We should bring gifts to this newborn king."

The three kings went off to prepare for the journey and when they returned, each had a precious gift for the Prince of Peace.

The first king sang out,

♫ **My gift is gold!**

and held up a beautifully decorated box full of gold.

The second king sang,

♫ **My gift is frankincense,**

♫ **And mine is myrrh.**

Sang the third king.

And the three kings set out to the west following the star.

♫ **We three kings of Orient are**
Bearing gifts we traverse afar
Field and fountain, moor and mountain
Following yonder star.

OHHHH, Star of wonder, Star of light
Star with royal beauty bright
Westward leading, still proceeding
Guide us to thy perfect light.

On and on they traveled. They grew weary and thirsty. They saw a small house, and the three kings decided to stop and ask to water their camels and to have a drink themselves. The first king knocked on the door. A girl opened it, and when she saw the three kings in their royal robes, she stepped back in amazement. She had never seen a king before. She called her mother, who invited the three kings into her house. They sat down at the kitchen table and enjoyed some fresh water the girl fetched from the well.

One of the kings asked, "Have you noticed the brilliant

star shining to the west?" The girl was too nervous to answer so she nodded her head. The second king asked, "Do you know why the star is shining so brightly?" The girl shook her head "No." The third king spoke, "The star is guiding us to the birthplace of a new king, the Prince of Peace. We are bringing gifts."

The first king sang out,

♫ **My gift is gold!**

and held up a beautifully decorated box full of gold.

The second king sang,

♫ **My gift is frankincense,**

♫ **And mine is myrrh.**

Sang the third king.

Looking at the beautiful gifts and picturing the Prince of Peace was overwhelming for the little girl. Then one of the kings asked her, "Would you like to go with us and see the newborn king?" The girl glanced at her mother. Her mother nodded and whispered, "You may go if you wish—a Prince of Peace is someone you should meet if you can."

The three kings stood up. "Good! We're glad you will come. Let's go!" "Wait," cried the girl, "I need a gift!" The second king shook his head, "You already have the greatest gift of all. Come. It's time for us to move on." The young girl did not know what the king meant, but she followed them out the door. She climbed up on the third king's camel and sat in front of him. They set out once more.

As they traveled, the girl looked up at the star and tried to imagine what this newborn king would look like. She pictured a great palace where they would see the royal child. Then she thought about the precious gifts that the kings were bringing and how she had nothing at all. Why did the king say, "You have the greatest gift of all"? She was confused and amazed at the same time.

Finally they came to the little town of Bethlehem. The star was now directly overhead, shining down into Bethlehem. The girl looked for a palace, but it appeared that there were no big buildings at all in this little town. She thought, "Maybe this is the wrong place." But she did not say a word as the kings rode through the streets and to the front of an inn. The girl thought maybe they would ask for directions or that they were stopping for some more water. They got down from their camels and the third king helped the girl to the ground. They walked around behind the inn and headed toward the stable.

The light from the star seemed brighter here than anywhere they had been. The girl wondered why the star was shining down on a stable instead of a palace. She was surprised when the kings tied up their camels outside. "The stable is for the camels," she thought. She followed the kings into the stable, and there she saw Mary and Joseph and the little baby Jesus lying in the manger. She knew right away that Jesus was the Prince of Peace. He did not need a palace. She looked up at the star shining down and the light filled her with wonder. Her eyes returned to baby Jesus.

The kings presented their gifts.

The first king sang out,

♫ **My gift is gold!**

and held up a beautifully decorated box full of gold.

The second king sang,

♫ **My gift is frankincense,**

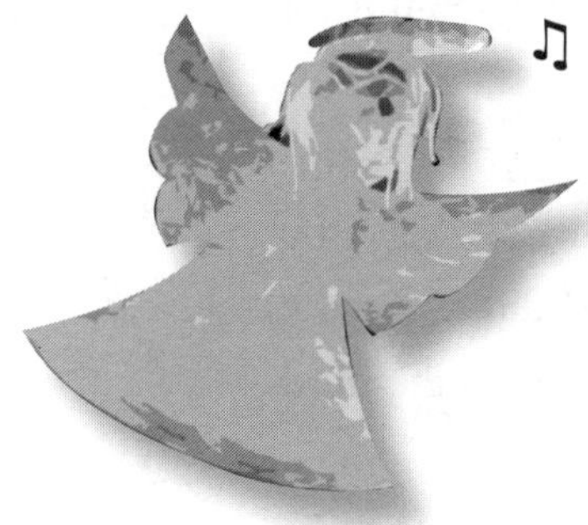

♫ **And mine is myrrh.**

Sang the third king.

Tears filled the little girl's eyes as she stared at her empty hands.

She said, "My gift is . . . ," She looked at baby Jesus. " Love," she whispered, and she kissed the newborn king on his forehead. "The greatest gift of all!" exclaimed the king.

AFTER THE STORY

And during times of gifts and giving, it is always good to remember that a gift from the heart is the greatest gift of all. And now we'll sing "Love Begins with Giving."

STORYTELLER TIPS

- You can invite everyone to sing along with you on "We Three Kings." It lets the whole group feel part of telling the story.
- The three lines of the kings describing their gifts are repeated three times. They may be sung (See refrain below) or spoken. It's fun to have three different people sing or speak the kings' lines.
- An alternative to this story: Instead of introducing the girl, have the kings enter Bethlehem and hear drumming "Pa-rum-pum-pum-pum." The kings go around a corner where they see a drummer boy dressed in ragged clothes. They invite him to come with them. Then have a guest sing "The Little Drummer Boy" song.

ART NEEDS

- The star
- Three kings
- Box of gold
- Frankincense
- Myrrh
- The girl
- Mary
- Joseph
- Baby Jesus in the manger

STORY SKELETON

- Baby Jesus is born.
- Three Kings in the East see the great star.
- They know it means a new king is born.
- They want to follow the star to the baby.
- They want to bring gifts.

My Gift Is Gold

(The Three Kings)

Bill Gordh

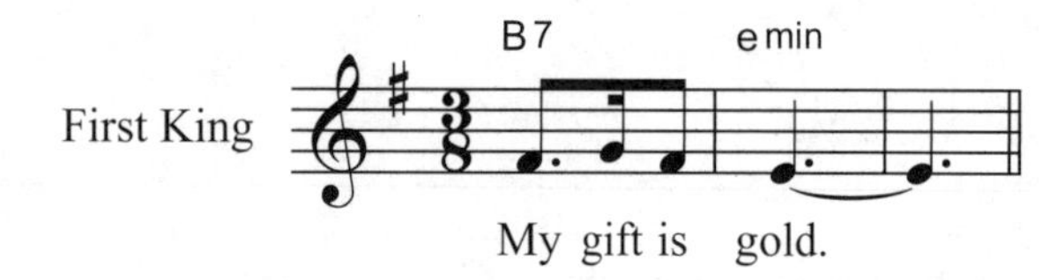

- They set out.

♫ "We Three Kings"

- They stop for water at a house.
- A girl greets them.
- She is amazed to meet kings.
- They tell her of their plans.
- They show her their gifts.

♫

- They ask her to join them.
- Her mother says, "Yes."
- She wants to go, but she has no gift.
- The king says, "She has the greatest gift of all."
- She doesn't understand, but she goes.
- She pictures the baby king and the palace he must live in.
- They arrive in Bethlehem.
- There are no palaces. She is confused.
- They come to an inn.
- They go to the stable.
- They see baby Jesus and Mary and Joseph.
- The kings present their gifts.

♫

- With tears in her eyes she says, "My gift is …"
- When she looks at baby Jesus, her heart fills, and she finishes her sentence, "love"
- The kings smile, "The greatest gift of all!"

chapter 28

THE PRODIGAL SON
LUKE 15:11-32

A Story about Forgiveness

Sing-along "Once a Brother" (p. 243) or "Amazing Grace"

The Prodigal Son story is a rich and layered story. On one hand there is the great celebration for the son who returns. There are also the hurt feelings of the dutiful son who watches the celebration for the brother who has caused so much trouble. Families are complicated organisms, and this story provides the basis for discussions about the relationships among siblings and parents. Names have been given to the brothers to make the story easier to follow.

BEFORE THE STORY

Today's story is one that Jesus told about two brothers. The artwork is by ___ ____ .

THE STORY

Everywhere Jesus went, he told stories. He called these stories parables, and they were both simple and complicated at the same time. The stories gave the listeners many things to think and talk about. One day he told a story about two brothers. It goes like this:

There was once a family with two sons. Jesus did not name the boys, but let's call them Caleb and Ezra. They were brothers but very different. Caleb helped around the house and worked hard on every job he was given. The father was proud of Caleb, and Caleb was proud of his work. The younger brother, Ezra, was very different. He thought Caleb was foolish to be working so hard. Ezra never helped and thought everyone should take care of him. He also got angry easily, and stormed off when things did not go his way. The father was a farmer, and there was lots of work to do around the farm, but only the one brother Caleb ever helped him.

One day Ezra came up to his father and said, "Father, I hate this farm. I don't want to be here anymore. Give me some money. I want to travel around and see the rest of the world." The father replied, "Son, come on, there is so much to be done here. You should help your brother. There are cows to be fed, sheep to be shorn; so many things to do. And one day, this farm will belong to you and your brother. There's no reason for you to leave."

But Ezra was not interested in the farm. "I don't want to be here, Father. I don't like the farm now, and I certainly don't want to live here after you are dead and gone! Give me some money now. You know you'll give it to me some day anyway. I'm ready to see the world!" The father looked at his son and gazed across the field where he saw Caleb hard at work. "Won't you go and help your brother. There is much to be done!" Ezra looked at his father, "Just because Caleb wastes his time working in the fields all day doesn't mean I should!" His father did not reply, and hoped Ezra would change his mind.

But the younger brother did not want to stay. He kept complaining and complaining and complaining. Finally his father agreed, "All right, my son, go out into the world. Here is some money. I hope you find what you are missing in life." Ezra took the money and left the same day. The older brother stayed on at the farm and worked and worked and worked.

The hard work in the fields showed. The farm's crops grew and grew and grew. It was a bountiful year. Caleb and his father were pleased with the results of their labor. The fields were full of corn. The cattle were healthy, and the sheep were busy taking care of the little lambs scampering across the grassy hills.

Now while the father and Caleb were working the farm, Ezra traveled to the city. He walked down the streets. It was exciting with so much more going on than out in the fields. Ezra liked the city. He found food he had never tasted, clothes he had never worn, and met all kinds of interesting people. Ezra made new friends. In fact when he showed his little bag full of coins, it seemed like everyone wanted to be his friend! He liked the attention of these strangers and paid for food and drink for everyone.

The parties went on night after night with Ezra paying for his new friends. Then one morning, he woke up and found that he had spent all the money his father had given him. There was not a penny left. It didn't matter Ezra thought. One of his new friends would pay for him for a change. He got up, washed his face, and went looking for one of his many new friends. When they realized Ezra had no money to pay for them, the friends turned their backs and walked away.

So Ezra went into one of the food shops where he had spent so much money, and asked for some food. The owner asked, "Where's your money?" Ezra answered, "I spent it all, but I'm hungry. Can't you spare a little?" The owner shook his head, "No money, no food." And as he walked out of the restaurant Ezra was thinking, "No money, no friends."

That night he walked the streets of the city, and no one seemed to know his name. Without any money, there was no place to stay, so he sat down outside and slept with his back against the wall of a closed shop. The next morning when he woke up, Ezra felt terrible. He had not slept well at all, and he was really hungry. He thought, "Maybe today I'll have better luck." But there was no luck for the younger brother—no luck, no friends, no food, and no place to sleep.

Ezra went hungry for a while, but finally got a job feeding the hogs for a farmer who lived just outside the city. As he slopped the hogs, Ezra thought, "I hate this kind of work, but at least I'll get some good food." But the farmer who hired Ezra was not like the boy's father who fed all his workers well. No, this farmer only gave the boy scraps to eat.

Ezra began to think about home. He pictured the hills and the fields and his brother and father sitting down to supper. He could almost taste the warm food and the fresh milk. Ezra realized he had made a terrible mistake. Maybe it was time to go back home. He could tell his father everything that happened. If he had to, he could take a job for his father. But then he remembered how he had said so many mean things to his father. He had made fun of his brother. He had laughed at their hard work and life on the farm. But Ezra did not want to stay at this terrible job, and he had nowhere to go—no money, no friends, no food, nowhere to go but home. He started walking.

Ezra walked and walked and walked. His clothes grew ragged. He had holes in his shoes. When he finally saw his father's farm, Ezra could barely walk. His father looked up from the plow. It did not even take a second for the father to recognize his son, even in his ragged clothes. He let the plow fall and ran, ran across the field to the road. He cried out, "My son is home. My son is home." Then he turned and called to the farmhouse, "Prepare a celebration!"

The father helped his son out of his ragged clothes and into a warm bath. After his bath Ezra came to the table. There was a feast, and the younger brother sat down. He whispered, "I don't deserve this." Caleb, the older brother, pushed back his chair and walked outside. The father followed him, "What's wrong?" he asked his older son.

Caleb answered, "Father, my brother was right when he said, 'I don't deserve this.' He doesn't deserve it. He took your money. He made fun of life on this farm and our hard work. He is only here now, because he has no place else to go." The older son continued, "Father, I have stayed here with you and worked by your side and watched the fields fill with corn. Still, you have never made a feast for me."

The father looked at his older son and said, "My son, you have stayed with me. We have worked together and all that is mine is yours. Every single meal we have together is a feast. And now your brother is home. He was lost. Now he is found.

He was blind to all that we were doing. But now he can see, and now he is here once again with us. Our family is back together. Come let us celebrate!" Caleb hugged his father, and they went back inside to have dinner with the prodigal son.

Jesus had finished the story and everyone was quiet thinking about it. Jesus always spoke of the love of God, and as they thought about the story, they realized that God loves everyone, and like the father in the story, will always welcome home the child who was lost.

AFTER THE STORY

And just like the family in the story, we embrace all you children here at ____ _____. The sing-along is "Once a Brother" (or "Amazing Grace").

STORY-TELLING TIPS

- Names have been given the two brothers to make the story easier to follow. If there are children who have either of these names amongst your listeners, change the names in the story.
- Sometimes the story is told with exclusive focus on the prodigal son. Following the feelings of both brothers, though making it more complex, is more compelling for the young listeners. It offers the wide range of feelings that every sibling goes through.
- Finding your own words of comfort for the older brother will make this part of the story more meaningful to the listeners, as they are already familiar with your warm and supportive tone.

ART NEEDS

- Father
- Caleb
- Ezra
- Something to represent the farm (corn, a sheep, a barn)
- Something to represent the city (buildings)
- Ezra's new friends
- Food for celebration (perhaps on a table)

STORY SKELETON

- Father and two sons live on a farm.
- Older brother Caleb works hard to make the farm flourish.
- Younger brother Ezra thinks it's a waste of time.
- Ezra asks for money to leave the farm and go to the city.
- After awhile, Ezra's father agrees.
- Ezra goes to the city and has lots of fun. He pays for everyone.
- When he runs out of money, his friends disappear.
- He has to find work.
- He gets a job slopping the pigs for a farmer.
- Farmer does not treat him well.
- Ezra realizes his mistakes.
- He decides to go home.
- The father stops everything and prepares a feast for his returning son.
- Caleb feels sad that he has always worked hard and never been celebrated.
- Father tells Caleb that every meal with him is a celebration.
- Father tells Caleb that his brother was lost and now is found and that is cause for the whole family to celebrate.
- The family celebrates.

chapter 29

JESUS AND ZACCHAEUS
LUKE 19:1-10

A Story about Friendship and Forgiveness

Sing-along "Love Begins with Giving" (p. 240-241)

The story of the small selfish man who climbs in a tree to see and hear Jesus suggests that everyone seeks to lead a kinder life if given the chance. The taking and returning of money is a notion even the youngest in our society are aware of, and since collecting taxes may be confusing, it is simplified in this story.

BEFORE THE STORY

Today we share a story of Jesus meeting a man who has been cheating his neighbors. The artwork is by _________ .

THE STORY

Zacchaeus was the tax collector in the town where he lived. He went from house to house collecting taxes from the people. The money went to the town to pay for things for everyone, like parks and roads. Every grown-up paid taxes. Zacchaeus was paid by the town to do his job, but he was greedy and wanted more money. He got an idea.

He decided to tell each person they owed more than they did. They would pay and he would keep the extra. So if someone really owed ten gold coins, Zacchaeus told them they owed fifteen. Then he kept the extra five gold coins for himself. Zacchaeus became one of the richest men in town, all because he cheated his neighbors. No one liked or trusted him, but they always paid their taxes.

It happened that Jesus was coming to town to tell his stories of sharing and caring and the great love of God. Everyone in the town was excited about Jesus' visit. That's all anyone was talking about. The question was—when would he arrive? Even Zacchaeus was interested.

The day finally arrived, and when Jesus entered the town, people crowded around to hear him speak. Zacchaeus saw the crowd. He wanted to see Jesus too. He was a small man and could not look over shoulders. He tried to push and shove his way through the crowd. This made people angry. Not only was Zacchaeus a cheat, he was rude!

Zacchaeus kept pushing, but the crowd did not let him through. He became desperate. What could he do? He really wanted to see Jesus. Zacchaeus saw a tree near by and got an idea. Zacchaeus climbed up the tree, and it was perfect. He could see Jesus and hear everything he had to say.

Jesus surprised Zacchaeus though. At the end of a story, he looked up into the tree and said, "Zacchaeus come down out of that tree." He looked at Jesus. He looked at the crowd. How did Jesus know his name? Jesus repeated, "I said, Zacchaeus, come down out of that tree." Zacchaeus was getting a little nervous, but he climbed down. Jesus walked over to Zacchaeus. "Now what?" he thought.

Jesus said, "Zacchaeus, I'm hungry. Could I have lunch with you today?" He looked at Jesus. Then he looked around at the crowd. He saw one of his neighbors. He knew she was always generous, sharing food with the hungry. Why didn't Jesus pick her? Then Zacchaeus saw another neighbor. The man was a carpenter and always did careful and honest work. Why didn't Jesus pick him?

Zacchaeus did not know what to say so he said, "Of course, of course. Come for lunch." The crowd moved aside, allowing Jesus and Zacchaeus to pass. Then the people, shaking their heads and confused, walked to their own homes for lunch. They did

not understand why Jesus went to lunch with the meanest and greediest man in town.

Jesus and the little man walked silently to Zacchaeus' house. They went inside. Zacchaeus set out his nicest plates and silverware. Then he brought out his freshest food. Jesus sat down and began to eat. Zacchaeus was too nervous to be hungry. All he could do was think, "Why is Jesus here? What is he going to say?" Finally Jesus spoke. He asked Zacchaeus about his life. He asked him about his job. Zacchaeus was always lying and cheating, but he could not lie to Jesus.

He said, "Jesus, I take more than I should. I cheat my neighbors and keep some of their tax money."

Jesus asked, "Why?"

"Because I want to be rich!" said Zacchaeus, "And I am. See my beautiful house and all my wonderful things!"

Jesus looked around and then asked, "Where are your friends?"

"Oh, I don't have any friends." replied Zacchaeus, "Nobody likes me. They all think I'm a cheat."

"I'm your friend," said Jesus.

"What?" asked Zacchaeus.

"I'm your friend," repeated Jesus.

Zacchaeus looked at Jesus. He looked into Jesus' eyes. He saw something he had not seen for a very long time—love. It was an amazing sight. Jesus smiled. In that moment, Zacchaeus knew all the things he had done wrong. He saw what his life was and what it could be. Zacchaeus spoke softly, "Excuse me, Jesus, but there are some things I need to do."

Zacchaeus ran out the door with a bag in his hand. Jesus looked out the window. He watched Zacchaeus knock on a neighbor's door. Zacchaeus was handing her money! He was filling both her hands. She was smiling. He was smiling too, a real smile that no one had ever seen. Soon though everyone saw his new smile because Zacchaeus did not stop with just one neighbor. He went door to door and to each neighbor he said, "I am sorry. I have treated you badly," and then filled his neighbor's hands with gold coins.

By the end of the day, he had a town full of surprised, new friends, and the townspeople understood why Jesus had chosen Zacchaeus for his lunchtime companion.

AFTER THE STORY

And here at _________we know the importance of being fair and taking care of our friends. The sing-along today is "Love Begins with Giving."

STORY-TELLING TIPS

- You may choose to have Jesus and the little man go straight to Zacchaeus' home after he climbs down from the tree. The idea of Zacchaeas looking around and thinking about other people provides an opportunity to give examples of neighbors who look out for each other, but is not crucial to the story.
- Consider using gold coin art to demonstrate on the felt board how Zacchaeas cheats. The visual will help children who might not follow the verbal description.

ART NEEDS

- Zacchaeus
- Jesus
- Bag of gold coins (optional)
- Tree
- Townspeople
- Table at Zacchaeus' house (optional)

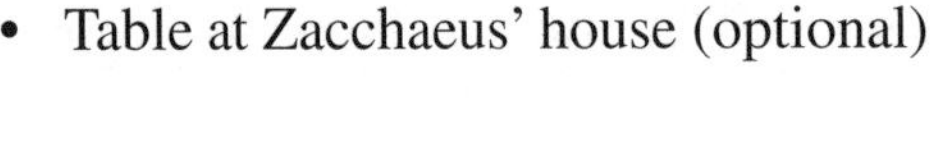

STORY SKELETON

- Zacchaeus is a tax collector.
- He cheats the people.
- He collects extra and keeps it for himself.
- Jesus comes to town.
- Everyone wants to see Jesus.
- Zacchaeus is small and can't see over the crowd.
- Zacchaeus climbs into a sycamore tree.
- Jesus sees him and asks to have lunch at his house.
- Zacchaeus agrees.
- Jesus asks him about his work.
- Zacchaeus can’t lie to Jesus and tells how he cheats.
- Jesus asks why.
- Zacchaeus says, “To be rich.”
- Jesus asks about friends and Zacchaeus says he has none.
- Jesus tells Zacchaeus that he is his friend.
- The love fills the heart of Zacchaeus and he is sorry for what he has done.
- He returns money to people.

part 7

NON-BIBLE STORIES FOR SPECIAL OCCASIONS

INTRODUCTION

Although this book focuses on a chapel program based on Bible stories, it is important to consider and include a variety of sources for your stories. In our program of thirty chapels for the school year, generally about nine of the stories are not from the Bible. One of the nine is always for Hanukkah. Another is in honor of Dr. Martin Luther King Jr. (MLK) and a third that is repeated most years is about St. Francis. Since these are common to many chapel programs, stories about them are presented in this section. In fact, two stories are offered for use in MLK programs.

The other stories we generally use for our chapels are drawn from world folktales. The presence of these stories in the program points out that we learn from many cultures. They demonstrate that in lands throughout the world, people share tales about taking care of each other, not giving up, and the importance of love and compassion. They also provide an opportunity to include more stories with female protagonists, even if it's just using "she" for the lead animal in the tale. There are numerous wonderful collections of folktales from all lands (I have over eight hundred volumes of folktales in my library) that you will find enthralling for you and the children you work with. But just as the Bible has many, many stories and only certain ones that resonate strongly with children, there are all kinds of folktales. You may need to read through quite a few to find those that support your chapel goals. Some authors (or collectors of tales) that you can rely on include Harold Courlander, Virginia Hamilton, Joanna Cole, Virginia Haviland, Verna Aardeema, Italo Calvino, Anne Pelowski, Diana Wolkstein, Joseph Bruchac, and Rafe Martin. I wrote a book entitled *Stories in Action: Interactive Tales and Learning Activities to Promote Early Literacy* (Libraries Unlimited) that contains forty folktales that you might find useful. Once you begin exploring these amazing tales, you may find, as I have, the joy of discovering stories from places you've barely dreamed of, much less thought of as potential for chapel content.

Another story source that many chapel programs incorporate is the picture book.

There are hundreds and hundreds of wonderful stories with dazzling illustrations that can be effective additions to any chapel program. Often the storybooks that are written specifically for an audience in a chapel setting are not the best stories. They have been written for the "lesson" the author wishes to teach rather than with attention to creating compelling characters, true emotions, and a meaningful plot. There are many fabulous authors whose stories will engage the children and offer substantial ideas to ponder. Go to such authors as Leo Lionni, Eric Carle, Tomie dePaola, Marie Hall Ets, Ezra Keats, and Jane Yolen. When you have found a picture book you like, consider telling the story with artwork made by the children.

chapter 30

HANUKKAH

REFERRED TO IN JOHN 10:22-23

A Story about the Importance of Faith

Sing-along "Hanukkah, Oh Hanukkah"

A story for Hanukkah is a part of many chapel programs and provides an opportunity to celebrate the importance of the freedom to follow one's faith. Although this telling includes fighting as a necessary response to the occupation of the temple, the focus remains steadfastly on the faith of the children of Israel, the miracle of the lamp staying lit, and the symbolic power of the flame representing the eternity of God's love.

BEFORE THE STORY

Beginning this Friday, many families will celebrate Hanukkah. Today we'll hear the story of that celebration. The artwork is by _______ .

THE STORY

Every year at this time of year we celebrate Hanukkah. We bring out the menorah and each night for eight nights add a candle. We use the number nine candle, called the "Shamas Candle," to light the others, one for each of the eight nights of Hanukkah. "But why do we do this?" you may ask. We answer this question by telling the story of the miracle of Hannukah.

Long ago in a city far away called Jerusalem, there was a big beautiful temple on top of the hill in the middle of the city. The temple was the place everyone gathered to sing and pray and gaze at the light coming from the lamp. The lamp was always lit, and it reminded everyone of the love of God, and how God's love goes on and on and on. But way back then, the people did not use candles. They used oil and little pieces of string called wicks. Each day they would add new oil to the lamp so the flame would keep burning. This is how it was for a very long time. Until …

Well, there was a king living in another land called Syria. His name was Antiochus, and he heard of this great temple in Jerusalem. He was told about the singing and praying and the lighted lamp that made people think of and feel the love of God. King Antiochus did not like the idea of this temple at all. He was king, and he decided to use his soldiers to wreck the temple and stop the praying and singing. He sent his soldiers to Jerusalem.

The people of Jerusalem watched with sadness as the soldiers marched through the city and up the hill to the temple. However, when the soldiers reached the temple, they could not tear it down, for it was made of great stones. So the soldiers ran off the people who were in the temple. Then they knocked over the benches and tore down the doors. They found the bottles full of oil and smashed them on the ground. Then they saw the lamp. The flame burned, but they did not take the time to really look at the lamp and the flame. They just blew it out and threw the lamp into a corner in the back of the temple. Then they brought farm animals into the temple as if it was a barn. The soldiers laughed.

The people at the bottom of the hill were not laughing though. They looked up the hillside to their temple, the temple they loved but could no longer go to. They were sad, very sad. And some of the children of Israel were not just sad, they were mad! So they met together and talked. They said, "King

Antiochus and his soldiers cannot tell us what to believe. It is our temple. These are our songs and prayers and we will get our temple back!"

These angry people with their leader, Judah Macabee, fought the soldiers, and after a long time, the soldiers left and returned to Syria. The happy people of Jerusalem ran up the hill to see their temple. What a sight! It was a mess! They looked at each other and declared, "We will make the temple ours again! Our songs will fill this space again!" So all the people, the mothers and fathers, grandmothers and grandfathers, boys and girls all worked together to make the temple beautiful again. They let the animals out, and they swept and scrubbed and cleaned. They picked up all the broken glass from the oil bottles. A sister and brother came running up. "We have found the lamp!" they said. Everyone stopped what they were doing and cried out,

"Light the lamp; light the lamp!"

They looked at the lamp. There was only a tiny bit of oil left, the rest of the oil ruined by the soldiers. They could not get more oil for eight days. What could they do?

"Light the lamp; light the lamp!" people cried.

"But it won't last," a grandmother said.

"Light the lamp; light the lamp!"

"But there will be no flame tomorrow or the next day."

"Light the lamp; light the lamp!"

The lamp had to be lit. For the people to feel that the temple was truly theirs again, they needed to light the lamp. And so they said their prayers, and they lit the lamp. The light shown and reminded everyone once again of the love of God and how that love will last forever.

The lamp stayed lit and not for just that one night. The next night when they returned to the temple, the lamp was still lit! It was impossible, but it was true. The lamp was still burning, and it kept burning for eight days. It was a miracle, the miracle of Hanukkah!

So we celebrate this amazing story from long ago by lighting the candles for Hanukkah, one for each night for eight nights. And when we look at the light of the menorah, we can remember this story and how the love of God goes on forever and ever.

AFTER THE STORY

And that is the story of Hanukkah. We will now sing "Hanukkah, Oh Hanukkah!"

STORY-TELLING TIPS

- Place a real menorah where everyone can see it. If Hanukkah has started, have the candles in place for that evening.
- The children listeners can make the sounds of the different animals as you tell of the Syrian soldiers bringing animals into the temple while placing the animals up on the felt board. They will have fun contributing the sounds. Acknowledging their fun while pointing out how sad it is for the people of Jerusalem allows their participation while allowing the emotional flow of the story to continue: "It sounds funny, but do you think the people in Jerusalem were happy about animals living in their temple? You're right. They were sad …"
- After you have said, "Light the candle; light the candle" a couple of times, invite the listeners to join the chant by saying, "And what did the people cry out?" Then repeat the chant with everyone.

ART NEEDS

- Temple
- Farm animals (in temple)
- Lamp with removable flame
- Boy and girl

STORY SKELETON

- Long ago in Jerusalem a great temple stood on the hill.
- People prayed and sang there.
- A lamp burned always.
- The flame reminded people that God's love goes on and on.
- The king of Syria, Antiochus, did not like the idea of the temple.
- Antiochus sent his soldiers to knock down the temple.
- The stone temple could not be knocked down, so soldiers wrecked it, tearing off the doors.

- Soldiers broke the jars of oil and threw the lamp in the corner.
- Soldiers brought farm animals into the temple.
- This made the people of Jerusalem sad.
- Some got angry.
- Judah Macabee was the leader of the angry people and they fought the soldiers.
- Finally the soldiers left.
- The people went back to the temple.
- It was a mess.
- Everyone helped clean.
- They found the lamp.
- "Light the lamp!"
- "There's not enough oil for it to keep burning."
- "Light the lamp!"
- They light the lamp.
- It burns for eight days.
- The miracle of Hanukkah.
- Now every year we light the candles to remember the miracle of the first Hanukkah and to remind ourselves how God's love goes on and on and on.

chapter 31

MARTIN LUTHER KING JR. CELEBRATIONS

Two Stories in Celebration

Sing-along "Amazing Grace"

Each January we have an opportunity to share some reflections on Martin Luther King Jr. and his legacy. The specifics of each community call for varied approaches to a special chapel in honor of Dr. King. The age of your children and the location of your church or school may make the presentation of some of the complex social issues a challenge. If the majority of the student body is Caucasian, that will add to the complexity of the planning for this chapel. The driving force in choices made for this chapel is inclusiveness.

For many years we told the story of John Newton, a white man who was a slave trader. When one of his ships almost sank with him aboard, he prayed for help and promised to give up trading slaves if he was saved. He was rescued, and from then on worked for the abolishment of slavery. He also wrote the beautiful song, "Amazing Grace." We closed this chapel by singing "Amazing Grace." It is a good story and seemed with our student body a nice way of showing how someone (a white) can work for others (blacks) when he sees people being unfairly treated. However, the connection to Martin Luther King Jr, other than his affection for the song "Amazing Grace," was not apparent.

One of our colleagues, Marie Fabian, spent a summer traveling down South retracing the route of the Freedom Marches of the '60s. Her journey included Atlanta and a trip to the childhood home of the King family. The home is owned by Ebenezer Baptist Church where Martin Luther King Sr. and Jr. both preached. Across the street Marie noticed a large concrete slab with a sign next to it. She crossed the street to read the plaque that described a store that once stood there, a store that was "Whites Only." So, even though the King family was a well-respected family in the neighborhood, and they lived directly across the street from the store, they couldn't go there for an ice cream cone. They had to go to a store further away. Years later, after integration, the city decided to leave the foundation of the building as a sad reminder of the past and a hopeful sign of change for the future.

Marie and a number of other colleagues felt we should address the issues of racism and King's legacy more directly than the John Newton story. Her experience offered a starting place for creating a new story. It would be a story based on the experiences of young Martin, one that would demonstrate that a child can witness injustice and see his future (much like Jesus did as a boy when he stayed behind in the temple). In our story we combined the whites-only store that was across the street with the one down the road. This "new" store would allow people of color to enter but only through the backdoor. This seemed like an elegant simplification that the children would understand.

BEFORE THE STORY

On Monday our school was closed. Does anyone know why? That's right. It was the birthday of Martin Luther King Jr.—a great American who believed everyone should be treated fairly and with dignity. This is a story about Martin as a young boy. The artwork is by _______ .

THE STORY

The Ice Cream Shop

Most of the stories we hear about Martin Luther King Jr. are about when he was grown up. But the ideas that grown-ups have usually start when they are children. This is a story about the young boy Martin. When he was a boy, just like all of us, Martin went to school every day. Every Sunday he went to church. First he went to Sunday school, and then he went to the big church for the service.

Martin always sat on the front row in the pew, so that he could hear every word spoken at the service. He loved listening to stories about the love of God. He also loved the Sunday service because the minister at his church was his very own father. He listened to his father's voice talking about a world of brothers and sisters filled with the love of God and of people respecting each other. Martin looked around the church and saw how everyone listened to those words his father spoke, and it made him proud! The whole experience filled his heart!

One Sunday after church, Martin asked his father if they could get an ice cream cone on the way home. His dad looked at Martin, smiled, and said, "Sure." You see, just across the street from Martin's house and down the street from the church was a little store that sold candy and pop and ice cream cones. So they walked to the store. When they got there, they saw some children lined up at the front door waiting for the store to open. Martin was surprised when his father led him right by the other children, past the front door, and around behind the building to the back door. They waited there for the store to open.

Standing at the back door, Martin had a strange feeling. He asked his dad, "Did I do something wrong?" "What?" asked his father. "Did I do something wrong?" repeated Martin. "No, Martin, you did nothing wrong. Why are you asking me that?" "Because," said Martin, "we're standing at the back door. We passed by all those children at the front door and we're at the back door. So I figure I must have done something wrong." Martin's father sadly shook his head, "You did nothing wrong, son. It's just the way it is right now. You see, the children at the front door are white kids. Martin, we're African American. We're black. They won't let us go through the front door."

"But that's not right, father. God loves everyone. That's what you always say at church." "That's true, son. God does love everyone." "And God doesn't care what color a person is," continued Martin, " or whether they are tall or short, straight hair or curly hair, skinny or fat. Right?" "Of course God doesn't care," said his father. "God loves everyone."

Martin looked at his Father. "Then it's not fair! Everyone should go through the same door! When I grow up, I'm going to help change those unfair rules. We can do better. We can overcome these problems!" Martin's father smiled at his young son. He was proud. He said, "That's a great idea and a noble undertaking. But for now would you like to go in and get an ice cream cone?" Martin looked at his father and shook his head, "I don't want an ice cream cone." They walked home—hand in hand.

That night Martin had a dream. And in that dream there were no back doors. Everyone worked and played and sang and laughed together.

♫ **We shall overcome.**
We shall overcome.
We shall overcome some day.
Deep in my heart
I do believe
We shall overcome some day.

We'll walk hand-in-hand.
We'll walk hand-in-hand.
We'll walk hand-in-hand some day
Deep in my heart
I do believe
We'll walk hand-in-hand some day.

And when Martin grew up, he did just what he said he was going to do. He became a minister like his father, and he talked about the power of love and respect for all people. When he saw that many of the rules were still unfair, he marched with his friends who felt the rules were unjust too. "No more back doors!" they cried.

When some would say, "Oh forget about those marches and peaceful ways. The only way to make things change is to fight those people that don't like us." But Martin looked at his angry friends and said, "Love is stronger than hate. Peace is stronger than war. We must love those who treat us badly, for only love can change their hearts and minds." Dr. Martin Luther King Jr. never gave up, and those rules were changed.

One Sunday afternoon when Dr. King was back in Atlanta, he walked to that ice cream store. There were people lined up waiting for the store to open, just like before. But no, it was different. *Everyone* was lined up at the front door—black and white and Asians and Hispanics as well. There was no one at the back door! He stood in line. When the store opened, he walked through the front door of that shop with everyone else and bought a chocolate ice cream cone. Mmm, did it taste sweet!

AFTER THE STORY

And we share stories of King's love and respect for all people every year at this time with the hope that we can help make his dream come true. Now we'll all sing "Amazing Grace."

STORY-TELLING TIPS

- Note that young Martin uses the word "overcome" when he is at the back door speaking of his dreams for the future. This introduces the word in a context that the children listeners will understand. So when they hear the song, it will make more sense.

- When you tell of King's dream, have a small group of faculty singing "We Shall Overcome," or if there are parents present, you can invite everyone to sing. If the children don't know the song, but hear their parents sing, it provides the basis for a family discussion later at home.
- When Martin returns to the ice cream shop, you can mix in the black, Hispanic, and Asian children to the line of people in front of the shop and comment on Martin seeing all the children lined up together.

ART NEEDS

- Martin Luther King Jr as a boy
- Martin's father
- Ice cream shop with front and back doors (or at least an indication of the front entrance)
- White children
- Black children
- Asian and Hispanic children

STORY SKELETON

- MLK Jr went to church and listened to his father's sermons.
- His father spoke of the great love of God and people working together.
- One day they went to the ice cream shop after church.
- Martin's dad led him past the children lined up at the front door.
- Martin and father stood at back door.
- Martin thought he was in trouble.
- Martin's father told him they were at the back door because they had black skin.
- Martin said it was not fair.
- Martin said he was going to help change things when he grew up.
- Martin said that these wrongs were things we could overcome.
- His father was proud.
- Martin did not want an ice cream cone anymore.
- Martin had a dream that there were no back doors and everyone worked and played together.

♫

- Martin grew up and became a minister.
- He tried to make his dream come true.
- He led marches when he found unfair situations.
- "No more back doors!"
- People said he should fight.
- He believed in peaceful change.
- Only love can change hate.
- Things began to change.
- Martin returned to the ice cream shop.
- Everyone was lined up at the front door.
- Martin lined up and then went into the shop.
- He ordered ice cream. Delicious!

Another Approach

Many people responded enthusiastically to the ice cream shop chapel, including written notes (not a common occurrence) expressing admiration for the care that was given to a difficult subject. However after a few years, we received another response—this one from an African American parent. Having heard about the Martin Luther King Jr. chapel beforehand, she decided not to bring her child but attend by herself. The chapel made her very uncomfortable, and fortunately she expressed her concern to the director. We met, and I pointed out to her how the ice cream shop experience showed how the young King's sense of unfairness led to the world beginning to see things differently. I added that it provided a wonderful model of a child's ability to notice things that are unfair, begin to think of the future, and decide how one can help make it better for others. She could not get past the imagery of the back door and the isolation it implied. With her son being one of the few African Americans in the school, she was afraid it would make a point of him being different and make him feel apart from the others. She suggested that the gathering should be a celebration and not such a heavy message chapel.

After a great deal of thought, my mind kept returning to the parable of the lost sheep, and it seemed that it was necessary to create a chapel that she would be proud to bring her child to. The following story is the result of this process. Having read and approved the story before the chapel, this parent brought her child. At the end, I looked over, and she gave me a big smile and a discreet thumbs up. Many other parents also commented about what a special story it was for this occasion.

BEFORE THE STORY

On Monday our school was closed. Does anyone know why? That's right. It was the birthday of Martin Luther King Jr.—a great American who believed everyone should be treated with dignity. Today we will share a story inspired by his dream—the hope that everyone will work and play together. The artwork is by ___________ .

THE STORY

The Land of the Color Curves

A story inspired by the dream of Martin Luther King Jr., by Bill Gordh

Sing-along "Work a Little Bit"

Once there was a world of curves and all the curves were the same shape, but they were not the same! Some were blue, others green, still others were red, and there were also the yellow curves.

Now in this world of curves, the Blue curves lived in the east, the Red in the west, the Yellow to the north, and the Green curves lived in the south.

Each color had its own stories and songs.

The Reds loved to work and that's what they sang about. In fact, that was the only word in their song. It went like this:

♫ **WORK, work, work, work**
WORK, work, work, work
WORK, work, work, work

The Greens like to gather flowers and put them in baskets. For a long time they sang the "Gather" song, but the word "gather" was too long a word for their song and so they started singing "Get" instead.

♫ **Get — get —**
Get — get —
Get — get —

The Yellows loved numbers and their favorite number was "2," so they sang the "2" Song.

♫ **2—2-2—2**
2—2-2—2
2—2-2—2

And finally the Blues. They had a laughing song that sounded like their laughter.

♫ **Her-her-her — her-her-HER**
Her-her-her — her-her-HER
Her-her-her — her-her-HER

Now this may sound all nice and peaceful with all these colors singing their songs and telling their stories, but it wasn't, because the different colors NEVER talked to each other. They did NOT want to know another color's stories or songs! So each color stayed in its own part of the land of curves and no one went into the middle. If a Red ever saw a Blue or heard the Blue's song, the Red covered its ears and ran home. The colors stayed clear of each other altogether.

But there was one little curve that just watched and thought about what it saw and heard. And one night this curve had an amazing dream about the colors being together. In the morning, it decided to see if it could make the dream come true.

It ran to a Red curve and told it the idea and asked if it would help—"OK" said the Red. It ran to a Green curve and told it the idea. "OK" said the Green curve. It ran to a Yellow curve. The Yellow curve hesitated. The little curve said, "Please, it will be fun. This afternoon. Please!" "All right," said the Yellow curve. Then the little curve went to the Blue curve and asked it to join the afternoon event. Blue answered, "I don't know. It sounds a little scary." "It will be fun," said the little curve. "And I'll let you be on the bottom." "Well, I'll try." "Great!" said the little curve.

Then the little curve told all the others to watch as the four colors climbed upon each other. Blue on the bottom. Then Green. Then Yellow and on top Red.

The other colors looked. What did they see? A Rainbow! And it was beautiful. All the colors loved the rainbow.

"Wait," said the little curve, "That's not all. Listen to them sing!"

Then the curve counted to four and the four colors began to sing. Each sang its color's song.

The Red

WORK, work, work, work.

The Yellow

2—2-2—2

The Green

Get — get —

The Blue

Her-her-her — her-her-HER

And as they sang, their songs became one song.

Work 2 get her

Work together!

It was an amazing four-color song! And all the other color curves liked this new combination song and began singing too!

And after that great afternoon, it wasn't long before you'd see a Blue curve and a Green curve and a Yellow curve sitting together listening to one of the amazing stories of the Red curves. And the next night they all listened to Blue stories, then Green, then Yellow. And they learned each other's songs! And then they started creating new songs and stories that were about all the colors. On top of all that, their world was bigger now because they happily played everywhere in the whole Land of Color Curves.

Now you may be wondering about that one special little curve, the one with the dream. Maybe you've been trying to figure out what color it was. Well, you see this story is from long ago and now that all the colors are friends, nobody seems to remember which color that curve was. If the Reds are telling the story, it seems that curve was red. If the Blues tell the story, then that dreamer curve was blue. But it really doesn't matter, does it? Because now they are all singing and working and playing together.

And you may say, "But we're not curves. So why did you tell that story?" And I like to think that if Dr. King heard this story he would answer the question for you. He might say, "It's true we're not color curves; we are all people. But like the curves, we're not all the same. Still, if we listen to each other's stories and sing each others songs, and learn to laugh and work and play together, we can all share a great big wonderful world!"

AFTER THE STORY

And here at ________ we try and make Dr. King's dream come true by listening to each other, and by working and playing together and showing respect for everyone. Now we will sing "Work a Little Bit."

STORY-TELLING TIPS

- This story is fun to do with some guest performers. Each of your guests can be one color (so four or eight guests). When you introduce each color's song, the designated color can sing with you (the song is really a chant and quite simple). Then when all four colors are chanting, you can have each color join in one at a time. As it is sung again and again, the new message will reveal itself.
- If you have the colors represented by four people, ask each to speak when the little curve goes around asking them to try out the idea. We had a color curve hanging on a string necklace for each guest—a nice visual support.
- With very young groups leave out the closing part about the color of the dreaming curve. It is not a concern and becomes a distraction from the point of the story. For older children, it is one of the questions that come to mind.

ART NEEDS

- Four red curves
- Four green curves
- Four yellow curves
- Four blue curves

STORY SKELETON

- There was once a land of color curves: red, yellow, blue and green.
- Each color had its own stories and songs.
- Red curve loved to work and sing.

Curve Song

(Dr. Martin Luther King, Jr.)

Bill Gordh

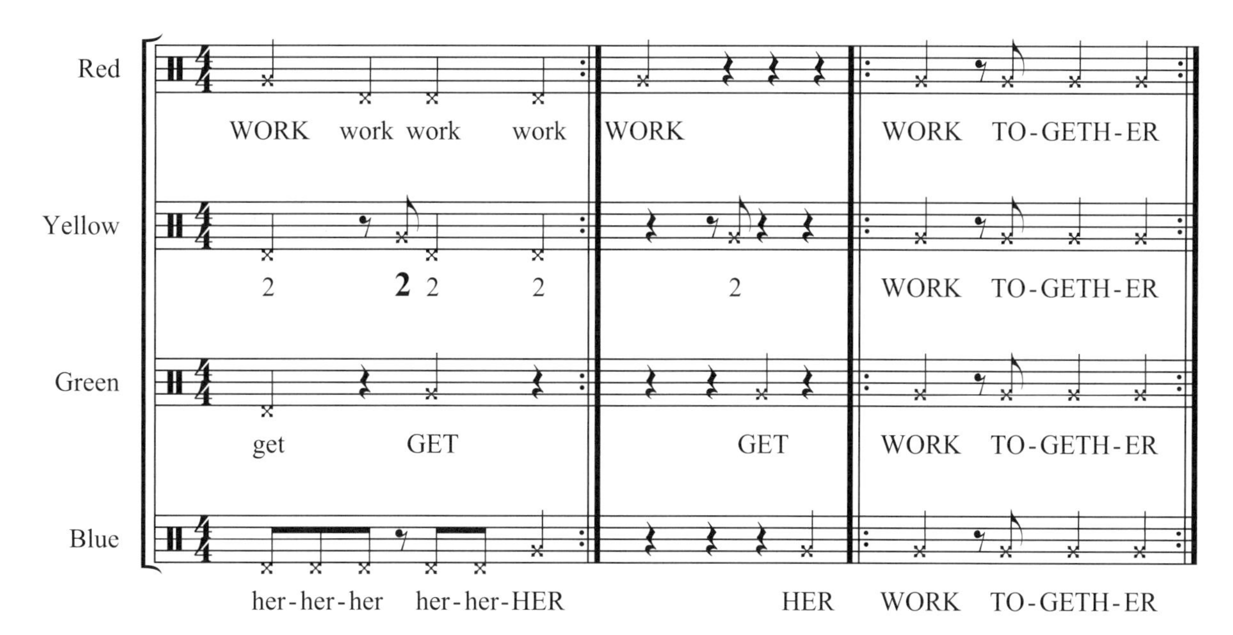

- Green curve gathered flowers. Shortened gathering to get.

♫

- Yellow loved numbers. Favorite "2"

♫

- Blue: Laughing.

♫

- They loved their own songs and stories, but they never got near any other color.
- The center of the land was empty.
- One night one curve had a dream.
- It dreamed that they were singing and working together.
- So it went to one curve in each group to ask if it would try out the idea.
- With some hesitation, they agreed.
- One climbed on top of another with Blue on the bottom, then Green, then Yellow, and then Red.
- They formed a rainbow.

- They started singing their songs.
- The songs became one song. "Work 2-get-her. Work together."

♫

- If someone asks the color of the curve who dreamed, each color is certain it was its color.
- It really doesn't matter, as now they all work and sing and play together.
- Why tell a story about curves when we are people?
- Curves are curves; people are people. But as in the story, there are differences. If everyone listens and works together, the differences only make us stronger.

chapter 32

SAINT FRANCIS

A Story Based on the Life of Saint Francis

Sing-along "Love Begins with Giving" (p. 240-241)

Many school and church programs include a blessing of pets in honor of St. Francis on or near his feast day on October 4. Some schools invite the children to bring their stuffed animals to get blessed! Still others do not specifically refer to the feast day but enjoy sharing a story of the man who was known to speak with animals. The story in this volume focuses on his transformation from a very self-centered person to one full of love for everyone. It's an opportunity to remind the young listeners to appreciate and care for the beautiful world we live in.

BEFORE THE STORY

Today's story is not from the Bible. It's a story from long, long ago about a man named Francis who lived in an Italian town called Assisi. The artwork is by ________.

THE STORY

The story today is about a man named Francis. When you hear about him now, he's usually called St. Francis of Assisi. When you see pictures of him, he is always with animals. They say he could talk to animals. But he was not always like that. In fact, when he was young he didn't like animals at all.

Francis grew up in a big house with plenty of everything. His parents had lots of money and gave him anything he wanted. They asked him if he'd like a pet. Francis said, "No. I don't want a pet. You have to take care of a pet. You have to feed it and pet it and give it water. I don't have time for that. I'm too busy taking care of me!" That's how Francis felt. He hardly noticed anything around him except a group of friends he played with. When he grew older and others were getting jobs, Francis did not work. He wanted to just goof around and go out every night. When he tired of a shirt or some pants, he just threw them on the floor and got something else.

Then Francis got sick—very, very, very sick. He climbed into his bed and lay there day after day after day. For a while, his partying friends stopped by. But Francis wasn't much fun anymore, so they went on their way. Then no one visited him at all, not even his parents as they were very busy. Well, almost no one visited Francis. He actually had one visitor—a little songbird that landed on his windowsill every morning and sang a beautiful song. Day after day, the little bird came, but Francis never paid it any attention.

But then one day, the bird was not there. There was no song, and Francis noticed. Lying in his bed, he stared across the room at the spot on the windowsill where the bird usually stood. Francis was worried. What happened to the little bird? And Francis realized without even knowing it that he *had* noticed the little bird; for now, he pictured the colors of the feathers and heard every note of its song. He missed the songbird and it got him thinking of all the things he had missed—like caring for others.

For the first time Frances closed his eyes and prayed,

♫ **I heard the birds sing,**
But I wasn't listening.
I watched the sun rise,
But I didn't see.
Though my heart goes on beating,
All my life I've been retreating
From so many things.
So please help me
Be the me I can be.

(Verse 2) **I walked a lone road,**
But I didn't know it.
I sang a sad song,
But nobody knew.

Though my heart goes on beating,
All my life I've been retreating
From so many things.
So please help me
Be the me I can be.

Chorus **For I can be kinder;**
I can be a reminder
Of how one can change.
So please help me
Be the me I can be.

He opened his eyes. He heard a little song. There, on the windowsill was his friend, the little songbird, and it was singing! Francis got up out of bed for the first time in months and walked slowly to the window. He did not want to frighten his little friend, and the songbird did not fly away. It jumped up onto his shoulder and together they looked out the window. It was like a new world to Francis: the blue of the sky, the soft puffy clouds floating along, birds winging their ways above the trees, people walking down the street. He saw some folks walking by dressed in rags. He called to them. They looked up at Francis, and he told them to wait. He went to his closet, took out all his clothes, and handed them out the window to the people waiting below! A new life had begun for Francis.

Soon he had new friends traveling with him as he spoke about the love of God to everyone he met—every man, woman, child, and animal. One of the new friends was Clare, and they worked together for a long time. (The story may end here.)

But more than the new people friends he met, Francis is remembered for the animals he loved. Yes, now he loved all the animals that he once had no time for. They say he could speak with animals, and they could understand him. And there are many stories of Francis and the animals. Here are a few.

One day Francis saw a flock of birds out in a field. He left the road and ran through the tall grass. His friends watched as Francis spoke with the birds. The birds did not fly away. They gathered around him, and he talked to them about how lucky they were to be part of God's amazing creation. "You get to fly through the skies and have those beautiful little birdies in your nest, all because of the love of God. Now fly away, birds, fly!" And off they flew.

Another time Sister Clare (Francis called his traveling friends "sister" and "brother") came to Francis with a rabbit she had freed from a trap. Francis took the bunny, set it in his lap, and spoke to it, "Now bunny, you must stay away from traps. Keep in the bushes or in the forest. That's where God made it safe for you. Now hop along." And he set the bunny down on the ground. The bunny jumped back into his lap. He set the bunny on the ground again, but once more the rabbit jumped into his lap. Finally he handed the bunny back to Sister Clare and asked her to set it free where it would be safe.

Another story tells of Francis setting free a fish. He wound up telling stories to the fish he freed and many other fish from the boat. There are pictures of all the fish with their heads sticking up out of the water. He spoke to them of the love of God and their good fortune to swim in the sea.

During his travels, he came to a walled town. The people in the town were frightened. There was a hungry wolf living in the woods nearby, and it had been attacking and eating their sheep. They were afraid it might attack one of their children. Francis spoke. "Come with me," he said. "We will go speak with the wolf." The villagers picked up clubs and started to follow. Francis turned and told them, "Put down your clubs. I go in peace." The villagers put down their clubs, but as soon as they got into the woods, they got frightened and ran back to the village. Francis and Sister Clare and a couple of other brothers and sisters traveled on.

Soon they saw the wolf. It looked hungry, and it bared its teeth and ran at Francis. He said a little prayer and calmly waited for the wolf. The wolf slowed down.

Francis watched the wolf as it calmly moved closer and rubbed against Francis's leg. He petted the wolf like a dog and spoke to it, "Now wolf, I know you are hungry, and you need to eat, but you should not frighten the people. We are all God's creatures, after all. I have an idea. If the people feed you, will you stop scaring them?" The wolf nodded its head and the stories say that the wolf shook Francis's hand with its paw! They returned to the village together.

When the villagers saw the wolf, they grabbed their clubs again, but Francis said, "Put down your clubs. The wolf will be your friend. If you feed it, it will not bother you." The story goes on to say that the wolf lived in the village for two years and only had to scratch on someone's door whenever it was hungry. It was always fed, and the wolf never bit a single person!

Francis continued his work. He was named a saint. When we think of Saint Francis, we remember his kindness, his love for all living creatures, and how we should think about others and not just ourselves.

AFTER THE STORY

The story of St. Francis reminds all of us to take the time to see the beauty in all the creatures in the world and to think of others. Now we'll sing "Love Begins with Giving."

STORY-TELLING TIPS

- The story can be told up to the break if you wish to have a shorter story that focuses more exclusively on Francis's conversion. If you wish to continue and tell the stories of Francis and the animals, you may wish to share those included here or pick one or two that suit your group.
- If you (or a singer in your group) are not going to sing the prayer in the story, you can read or recite part of it or substitute your own.

ART NEEDS

- Francis
- Human friends
- A bed
- A singing bird
- Woman friend (Clare)
- Wolf
- Other animals (friends of Francis) can include fish and birds

STORY SKELETON

- Francis had a big house. His parents were wealthy.
- He did not want a pet—too much work.
- Frances grew up but never worked.
- He stayed out late with his friends.
- Francis got very sick.
- His friends stopped visiting.
- A songbird was his only visitor.
- Francis did not notice the little bird.
- One day, songbird was not there.
- Now Francis missed the bird.

I Heard the Birds Sing

(The Story of St. Francis of Assisi)

- He became sad about how he had misused his life.
- Francis prayed.
- The bird came back.
- Francis got out of bed.
- Francis was ready to start a new life.
- Francis gave away his clothes.
- Francis now loved all animals and could speak with them.
- Francis talked to a flock of birds about their good fortune to be birds and how they should be thankful.
- Francis freed a trapped bunny and sent it on its way.
- Francis spoke with fish from his boat.
- Francis came to a town that was being frightened by a wolf.
- Francis went looking for the wolf.
- It started to attack.
- Francis prayed and the wolf did not attack.
- Francis petted the wolf.
- Francis befriended the wolf.
- The wolf became the pet of the village.
- Francis was made a saint and is remembered as the friend of animals.
- Francis reminds us to think of others.

part 8

THE SONGBOOK

INTRODUCTION

Our songbook at The Episcopal School in the City of New York is divided into five sections: Bible Story Songs; Sharing and Caring; Working and Working; You and Me; and Holiday Songs. They are listed below with the songs I wrote in bold. The lyrics and music to these songs follows this listing. A number of excellent songs are suggested which are traditional songs or were written by other songwriters. They are wonderful songs you might consider for your own songbook and are not difficult to track down. The songs have been set in keys that are in a good range for young singers.

The songs in **bold** are included in this book with lyrics and music.

- **Now Is the Time** (Chapel opening song)

BIBLE STORY SONGS

- Arkie, Arkie (Traditional)
- Daniel in the Lion's Den (Traditional)
- Go Down, Moses (Traditional)
- Joshua Fit the Battle of Jericho (Traditional)
- Little David Play on Your Harp (Traditional)
- One More River (Traditional)
- **Peter and John and James (Bill Gordh)**
- Rock-a-My Soul (Traditional)
- Sons of Father Abraham (Traditional)
- Who Did Swallow Jonah? (Traditional)

SHARING AND CARING

- All God's Children Have a Place in the Choir (Bill Staines)
- All Thing Bright and Beautiful (Traditional with words by Cecil Alexander)
- **I Want to Thank You (Bill Gordh)**
- Kumbaya (Traditional, African American)
- **Love Begins with Giving (Bill Gordh)**
- Love Is Something if You Give It Away (Malvina Reynolds)
- Michael Row the Boat Ashore (Traditional, Georgia Islands)
- My Nipa Hut (Traditional, Philippines)
- **Once a Brother, Always a Brother (Bill Gordh)**
- This Land Is Your Land (Woody Guthrie)

WORKING AND WORKING

- **In My Garden (Bill Gordh)**
- **Keep on Trying (Bill Gordh)**
- Simple Gifts (Traditional)
- **Sow Your Seeds (Bill Gordh)**
- The Garden Song (Dave Mallet)
- We All Work Together (Woody Guthrie)
- **Work a Little Bit (Bill Gordh)**

YOU AND ME

- A Little Less of Me (Glen Campbell)
- Amazing Grace (John Newton)
- **A Snake Named LaRue (George Wurzbach)**
- **Everything Counts (Bill Gordh)**
- **I Heard the Birds Sing (Bill Gordh)**
- Little Wheel a' Turning (Traditional)
- This Little Light of Mine (Traditional) or This Little Candlelight of Mine
- You Are My Sunshine (Jimmy Davis and Charles Mitchell)
- **You Can Sing about Anything (Bill Gordh)**
- You Can't Roller Skate in a Buffalo Herd (Roger Miller)
- **You've Got Me (Bill Gordh)**

HOLIDAY SONGS

- Away in a Manger (Traditional)
- Birthday Song (Woody Guthrie)
- Children, Go Where I Send Thee (Traditional)
- Feliz Navidad (Jose Feliciano)
- Gloria (Traditional)
- Hanukkah, Oh Hanukkah (Traditional)
- Silent Night (Traditional)
- The Dreidel Song (Traditional)
- **The Very First Christmas (Bill Gordh)**

Now Is the Time

Bill Gordh

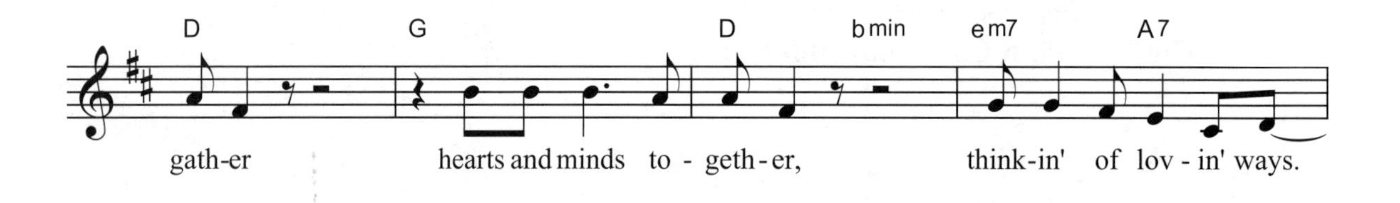

Peter and John and James

(Jesus and the Fishermen)

Traditional

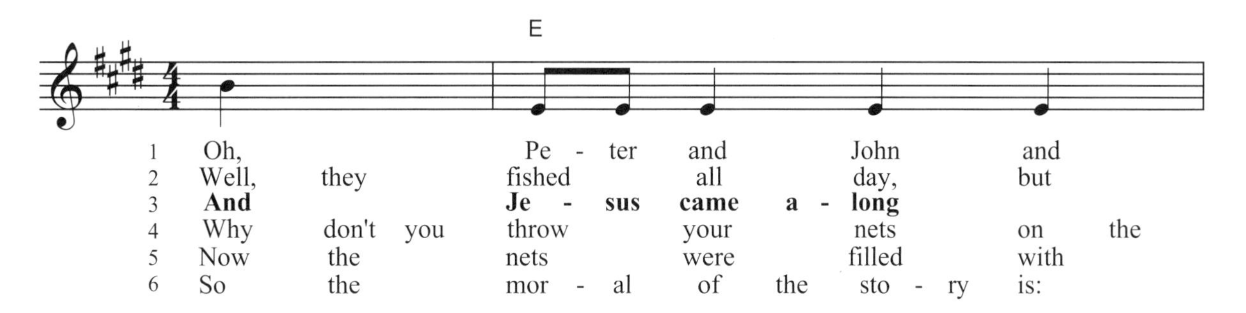

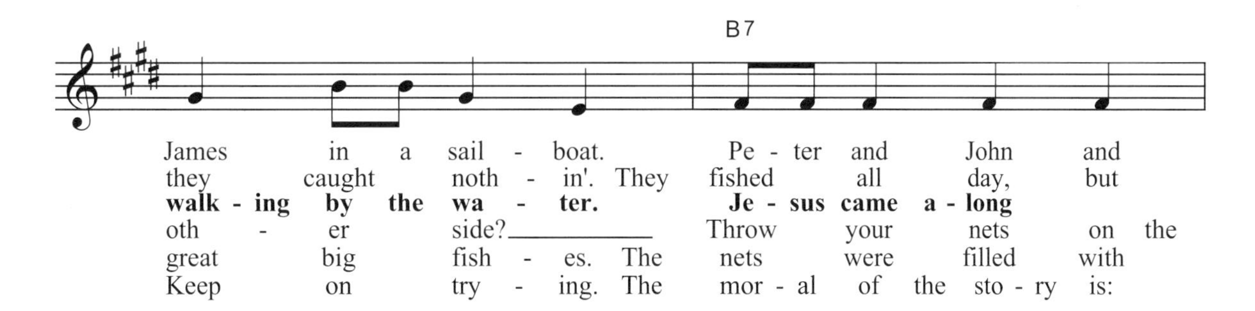

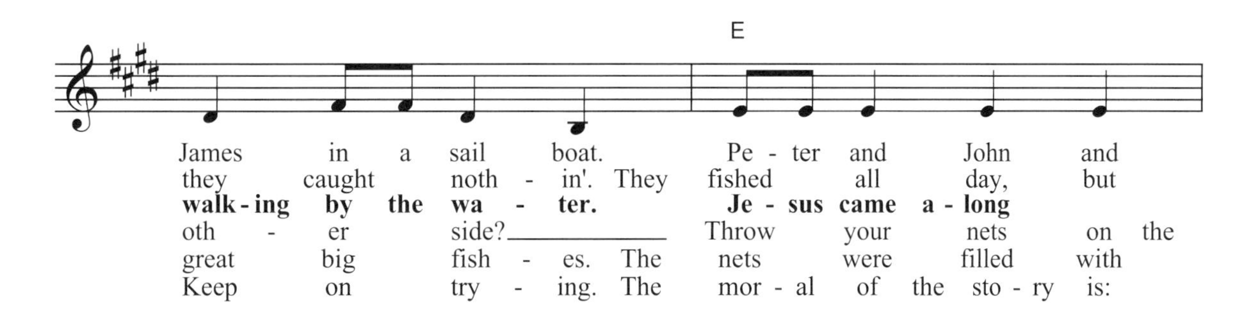

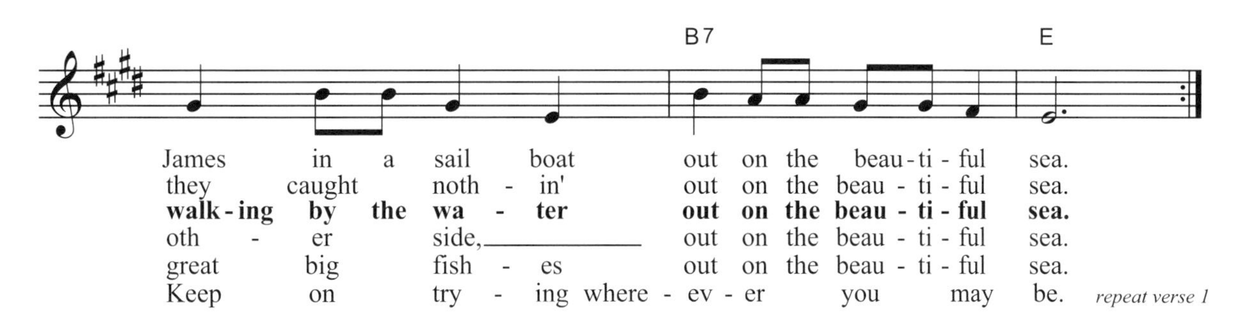

Verse 3 is bold to be a visual aid.

I Want to Thank You

Everything Counts

Bill Gordh

Love Begins with Giving

Bill Gordh

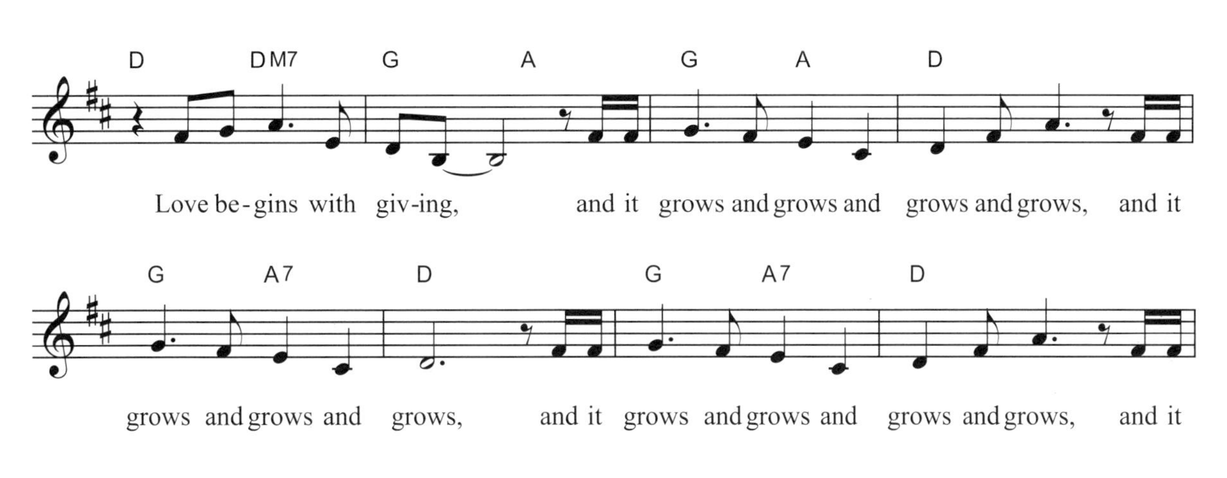
D DM7 G A G A D
Love be-gins with giv-ing, and it grows and grows and grows and grows, and it
G A7 D G A7 D
grows and grows and grows, and it grows and grows and grows and grows, and it

G A D
grows and grows and grows.

Work a Little Bit

Bill Gordh

If you're in a hurry,
You don't have to worry,
'Cause I'll give you a hand,
Knowing we'll be working side by side.
Put our heads together
In any kind of weather.
We'll think up a plan
Workin' and workin' while smilin' a smile.(Chorus)

Once a Brother, Always a Brother

(Story of Joseph)

Bill Gordh

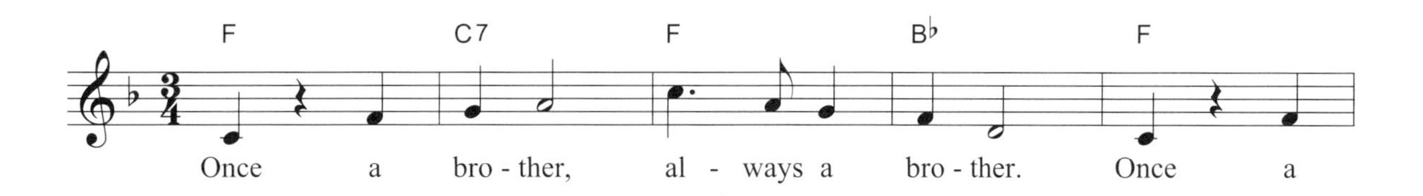

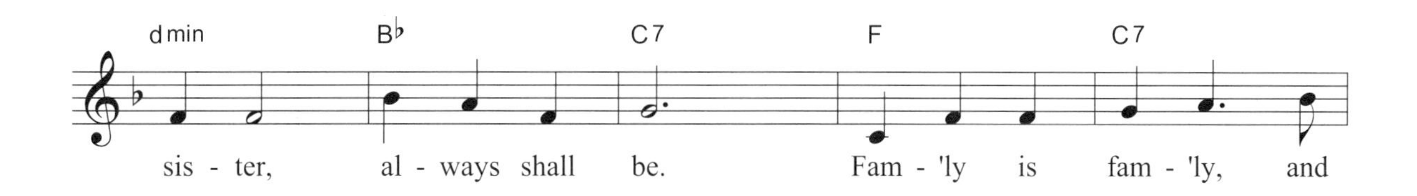

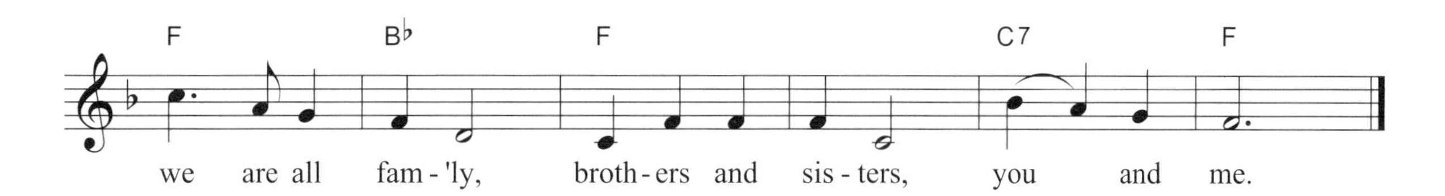

In My Garden

Bill Gordh

D
G
D
gar - den. And we'll weed out the weeds, and the stones we don't need; a
gar - den. And we'll weed out the weeds, and the stones we don't need; a
G
D
A7
few more seeds, and soon it's all green in my gar - den.
few more seeds, and soon it's all green in your gar - den.
D
A7
Flow-ers grow-ing tall in my gar - den.
Flow-ers grow-ing tall in your gar - den. There'll be flow-ers grow-ing
D
A7
D
tall in my gar-den. There'll be flow-ers grow-ing tall in all the gar-dens.

I Heard the Birds Sing

(The Story of St. Francis of Assisi)

Keep On Trying

Bill Gordh

It may come the next second
Or it might be an hour
It could take a year or three
But I'll tell you one thing
Sort of a warning
Try or it never will be. So,

(Chorus)

Sow Your Seeds

(The Parable of the Sower)

Bill Gordh

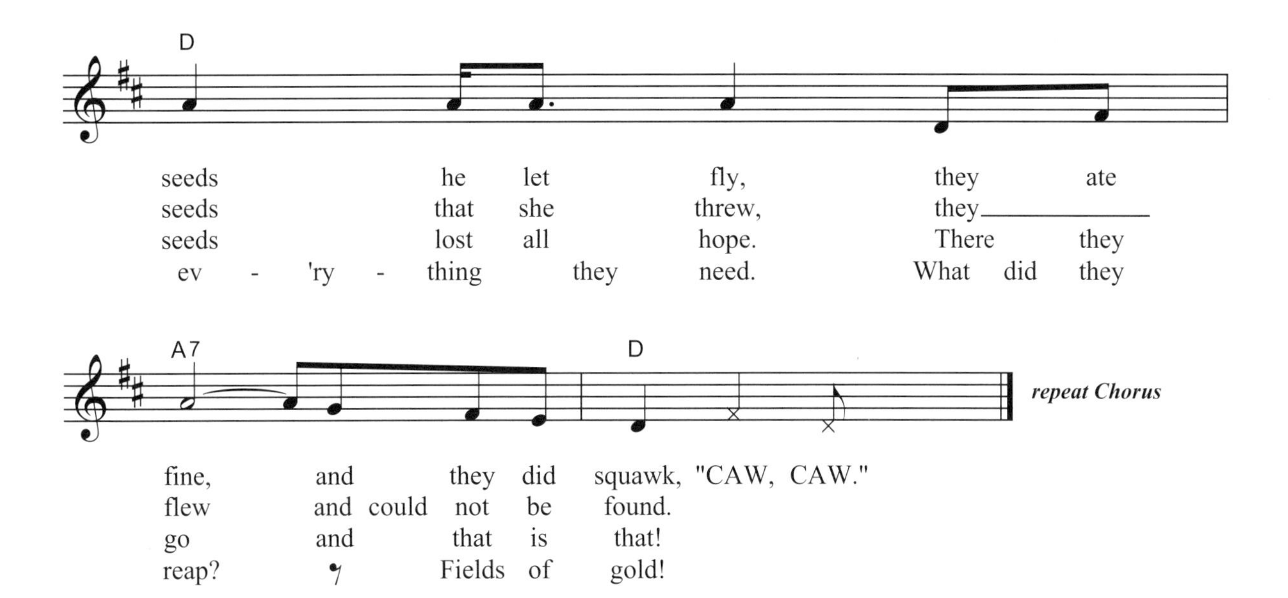
D
seeds he let fly, they ate
seeds that she threw, they
seeds lost all hope. There they
ev - 'ry - thing they need. What did they
A7
D
repeat Chorus
fine, and they did squawk, "CAW, CAW."
flew and could not be found.
go and that is that!
reap? Fields of gold!

A Snake Named LaRue

George Wurzbach

10 D G
crea-ture, to be ab-le to fly up so high where no-one can
12 D G
reach you. and a snake in the grass is sure-ly God's low-li-est
14 D A7 bmin A7 D G
crea-ture, and God must-n't like me 'cause I on-ly slith-er, slith-er.
16 D A7 G D
Look how you fly, while I on-ly slith-er!" The
18 D A7 bmin A7
bird took La - Rue in his claws.
19 D A7 bmin A7
Gent - ly he lift - ed and soared through the sky; they were
20 D G D A7 G
fly-ing, fly-ing! Be - fore La-Rue knew it the bird had him

22
D
fly - ing. And the
23
G
D
bird said, "La-Rue, you were there on the ark with No-ah. If
25
G
God had thought less of you, you'd have been left on the
26
D
G
shore. Here in the King-dom, there is no high-er or
28
D
A7
bmin
A7
low - er. Though I'm a - ble to fly it's just my way to
29
D
G
D
A7
G
slith-er slith-er. And I slith when I fly, and you fly when you
31
D
A7
bmin
A7
slith - er." La -

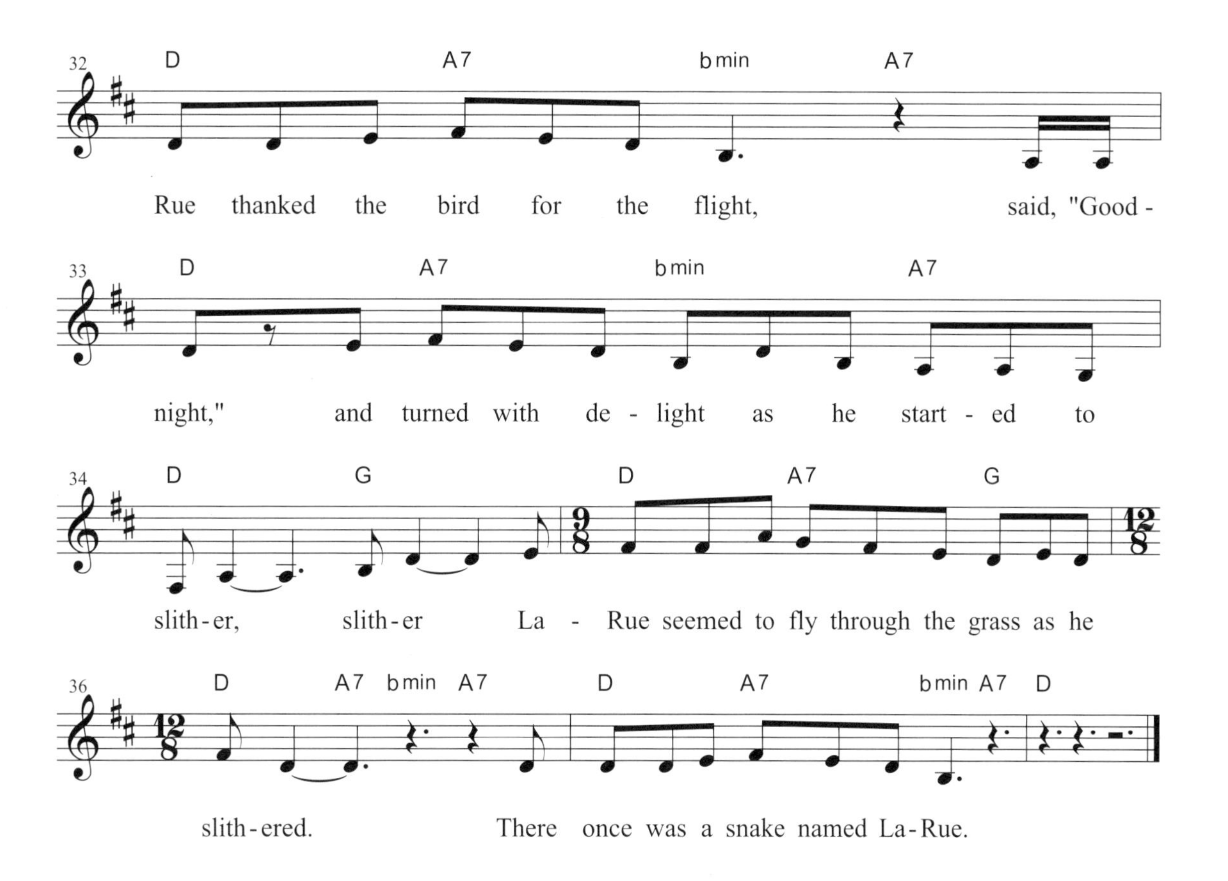
32
D A7 bmin A7
Rue thanked the bird for the flight, said, "Good -
33
D A7 bmin A7
night," and turned with de - light as he start - ed to
34
D G D A7 G
slith - er, slith - er La - Rue seemed to fly through the grass as he
36
D A7 bmin A7 D A7 bmin A7 D
slith - ered. There once was a snake named La - Rue.

Violin

A Snake Named LaRue

George Wurzbach
Violin obbligato by Christopher Minarich

23 G D
25 G D
27 G D A7 b min A7
29 D G D A7 G
31 D A7 b min A7 D A7 b min A7
33 D A7 b min A7 D G
35 D A7 G D A7 b min A7
37 D A7 b min A7 D

You Can Sing about Anything
Bill Gordh
A D A
You can sing a-bout the moon; you can sing a bout a star. You can
E7
sing a - bout a bus, a truck or a car. You can
A D A D
sing a-bout a mon-ster in the dark; you can sing, you can sing a-bout an-y-thing,
A E7 A
sing, sing, sing a-bout an - y - thing. You can
D A
sing a - bout a tree grow - ing up so tall, you can
E7
sing a - bout a flea that's oh so ve - ry small, you can
A D A D
sing a-bout big, or no-thing at all, you can sing, you can sing a-bout an-y-thing,
Copyright 2007 Bill Gordh

A E7 A
sing, sing, sing a-bout an - y - thing. When you're
D A D A
hap - py or ex - ci - ted, feel - ing lone - ly, scared or blue, what-
D A B7 E7
ev - er's go - in' on in - side, well, you can sing a-bout that too, You can
A D A
sing a - bout the hills; you can sing a - bout the sea. You can
E7
sing a - bout cats and birds and bum - ble bees. You can
A D
sing a - bout you bro - ther or your sis - ter or me; you can
A D A E7 A
sing, you can sing a-bout an-y-thing, sing, sing, sing a-bout an-y - thing. You can
D A E7 A
sing, you can sing a-bout an - y - thing, you can sing, sing, sing a-bout an-y-thing.

You've Got Me

Bill Gordh

The Very First Christmas

Bill Gordh

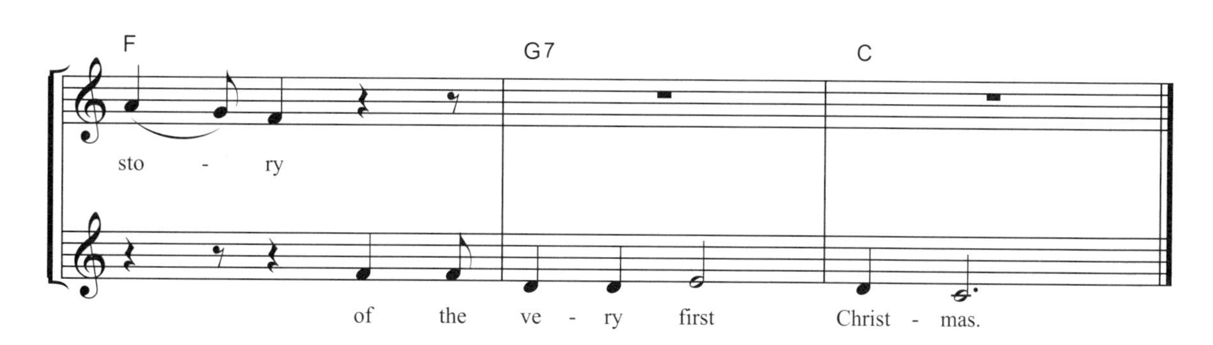

2 Leader Well, the angel came to Mary.
Group The angel came to Mary.
Leader Said, you're gonna have a baby
Group On the very first Christmas.

3 Leader And Mary spoke to Joseph.
Group Mary spoke to Joseph.
Leader She said, I'm gonna have a baby
Group On the very first Christmas

4 Leader Now they're on the road to Bethlehem,
Group On the road to Bethlehem,
Leader But there is no room at the inn
Group On the very first Christmas.

5 Leader But there's room back in the stable.
Group There's room back in the stable.
Leader And there they'll find a manger
Group For the very first Christmas.

6 Leader And Mary had her baby.
Group Mary had her baby.
Leader And she named that baby Jesus
Group On the very first Christmas

7 Leader Baby Jesus a-sleeping,
Group Baby Jesus a-sleeping,
Leader And peace the world is keeping
Group On the very first Christmas.

Tag Leader And peace the world is keeping
Group On the very first Christmas.